General Education

A Symposium on the Teaching of Non-specialists

Edited by MICHAEL YUDKIN
With a Foreword by SIR ISAIAH BERLIN

ALLEN LANE THE PENGUIN PRESS

Copyright © Michael Yudkin
and Contributors, 1969

First published in 1969

Allen Lane The Penguin Press
Vigo Street, London W1

SBN 7139 0115 2

Printed in Great Britain by
Butler & Tanner Ltd, Frome and London

Set in 11 on 13 pt Monotype New Times Roman

Contents

Editor's Preface   vii

Foreword, Isaiah Berlin   ix

English, Reuben Brower   1

History, J. D. Heydon   28

Sociology, Jennifer Platt   52

Mathematics, Alan Tayler
            Alan Tammadge
            Philip Prescott   76

Experimental Science, Michael Yudkin   114

Philosophy, Bernard Williams   138

Conclusion, A. D. C. Peterson   165

Editor's Preface

UNDERGRADUATE education has customarily been more specialized in England than in many other countries. The tendency away from specialization began only recently, and in the newer foundations; but it has spread far enough that Oxford University (for example) now has Schools in Engineering and Economics, Physics and Philosophy, and other combinations. In some universities, a main field of study is accompanied by others which may be fairly unrelated to it; and in others, a comparatively specialized honours course is preceded by a year of much more general study.

But whatever the precise pattern, the teaching of a discipline to undergraduates that are not, and are not intending to become, specialists in it poses exceptional problems. What should be the content of such a non-specialist course? What should be its methods? How far can a course designed for specialists serve also in general education? It is in response to this kind of question that the present writers propose some tentative suggestions.

Tentative suggestions, not definitive answers. There is too little knowledge and experience in this area for us to claim that our proposals are more than starting points for discussion and for experiment. And whereas the aims of specialist education are usually fairly well agreed, the aims of general education are not always so clear. As A. D. C. Peterson points out in his concluding essay, the educational argument is in part an epistemological argument: what are the 'forms of knowledge' that students ought to be taught to appreciate, and in which of the

EDITOR'S PREFACE

traditional 'subjects' are they best exposed? The contributors to this Symposium have not explicitly discussed this problem; and although they have tried to show why the subjects that they write about are suited to general education, there is no implicit claim that others might not serve instead.

I none the less hope that these essays will stimulate some interest and provoke some debate about the function of general studies in higher education, and about the form it might take. Non-specialist studies will become increasingly common in the future, and will increasingly demand the time and the considered attention of university teachers.

MICHAEL YUDKIN

Foreword

ISAIAH BERLIN

This book consists of essays by a number of university teachers who seem agreed that education, even if it cannot by itself knock down the barriers by which human beings are divided, should at any rate not add to them. They believe that, whatever else the task of education, it should not drive the intellect and the imagination of students into channels that seem to become narrower as our century grows older; consequently, that it should do everything possible to make it easier for those engaged in one discipline to understand the methods, achievements, hopes, ambitions, frustrations, the intellectual and emotional processes, of those working in other fields. They know well the familiar obstacles to this: the disparity of subjects and methods, the fact that some persons are temperamentally uninterested in, or unfitted for, uncovering the secrets of nature; or disinclined to investigate how men came to be what they have become; or averse to, or incapable of, analysing the concepts and categories of thought or imagination, or reflecting critically on what is and what is not worth doing or thinking or being. Moreover, students do need to be qualified for professions, and this entails some degree of specialization, without which there can be no skills or knowledge or, save in exceptional cases, any intellectual discipline at all.

None the less, wider knowledge is worth striving for. It is not necessary to believe that all knowledge always makes men happier or freer or morally better. The applications of modern science, it may be argued, have increased oppression, danger, misery in some spheres, as well as vastly diminished them in others. It need only be accepted, firstly, that the discovery of the truth is a great good in itself; and secondly, that the only real remedy for the evil consequences, whether of ignorance or of knowledge, is more knowledge: clearer understanding of what is involved, of what is worth pursuing, of means and ends, consequences and their value. Unless men are given the chance to find out what kind of world they live in, what they have made, are making, and could make of it – and this can only be done if they have some notion of what other men are thinking and feeling and doing, and how and why – they will continue to walk in darkness and be faced by the unpredicted and sometimes appalling consequences of one another's activities – faced by this beyond the degree which seems inescapably imposed on us all by our imperfections. The fact that we are never likely to know enough is no reason for not seeking to know as much as we can; to settle for less than this is gratuitous defeatism: blind surrender to forces which can be controlled.

To come down from these high general principles to the concrete educational problems faced by the contributors to this book: if they establish any case at all – and they seem to me to do a good deal more than this – the difficulties are not insuperable. Alliances between cognate subjects in British universities – say politics and economics, or history and literature, or philosophy and physics, or those other recognized combinations which our less hidebound academic establishments permit – have always been feasible. But more doors can be opened: even if the student cannot be expected to proceed through more than a very few of these – and he would usually be ill-advised if he did – he can at least be encouraged to look out upon vistas which would do much to liberate him from the narrow confines in which at present he seems to be expected to exist. If even half of what the writers of these essays advocate proves feasible, much waste and nonsense can be avoided, and much positive harm too: in particular, liability to systematic misunderstanding of others and of oneself and of one's world past and present, and, connected with this, philistinism, much (often resentful) boredom, irrational fears and hatreds of forms of knowledge (and of life) which are felt to be alien, puzzling, and therefore hostile, with a consequent tendency to absurdities in theory which at times lead to barbarities in practice.

The educational problem is not new: it has been in the forefront of interest since at least the days of Comenius. The last three centuries are full of controversy about what it is that will produce the widest understanding, the fullest human life. Such controversy has been particularly lively in the United States; and if the writers of this book do not regard the general education courses or 'core subjects' provided in a good many American universities as examples of unqualified success, this does not mean that they do not appreciate the difficulties or the achievements of the educators of, say, Harvard or Chicago or Columbia, in particular their eagerness to make it possible for students to escape out of ancient strait-jackets towards a freer intellectual life. The mere proliferation of remedies is a symptom of the reality of the disease.

If this is true, then the recommendations in this book are worth examining, and indeed trying out too. At best they will do a great deal of good, at worst very little harm. They are founded on what seems to me a just appreciation of the situation in Britain at present.[1] In what follows I shall assume with (I believe) the writers of this book, that to understand the world in which we live is (for the reasons given above) good rather than bad; that most men cannot achieve this without much conscious effort or, as a rule, without help, in particular the help of teachers; and therefore such obstacles to this process as indolence, ignorance, dogmatism, obscurantism, active dislike of the intellect and rational argument, hatred of novelty, and especially jealous fear of neighbouring disciplines suspected of expansionist ambitions, are vices to be exposed and fought. I shall assume also that human beings are in general entitled to have their capacities for thought and feeling developed even at the cost of not always (or even often) fitting smoothly

[1] Written in the early summer of 1968.

into some centrally planned social pattern, however pressing the technological demands of their societies; that public virtues and social peace are not necessarily preferable to, still less identical with, the critical intellect, the unfettered imagination, and a developed capacity for personal relationships and private life. To these ends education, and in particular university education, can and should be a powerful means, or, at least, not a positive hindrance.

What are the characteristics of our time to which education should be made relevant? Let me add one or two further truisms. Educational needs spring from the pattern formed by the permanent – or, at any rate, relatively widespread – needs of human beings, modified by the predicament of the particular society in which they live. To understand his needs a man must know something of the times he lives in – here is a truism if ever there was one; yet it is, at times, ignored or else interpreted too narrowly. When the present century comes to be viewed from some relatively remote and calm perspective – say a century or two after our time, if humanity survives till then – our age, it seems to me, will be notable not for a revolution in the visual arts and sensibility, like the Italian Renaissance; nor for the rise of bold and ruthless individualism; nor for optimistic faith in the new weapons of reason and empirical science; nor for the achievements of poets and novelists; nor for belief in the liberating powers of science or democracy; nor for mounting expectation of universal peace, harmony and the progress of all mankind under the rule of a wise, beneficent and gradually widening *élite*. It seems to me more likely that the salient characteristics of our age will be attributed to two phenomena: on the one hand, the Russian Revolution and its consequences; and, on the other, the unparalleled progress of natural science and its applications to human lives. These developments of western civilization have dwarfed all others, and have radically altered and are still transforming the entire world. Yet to some degree they are in conflict with one another. On the one hand they have led to increased belief in reason, and, in its name, in destruction of privilege rooted in irrational convictions, resistance to traditionalism and to transcendent and impalpable values – all that goes by the name of the faith of the Enlightenment. This has given birth to egalitarian principles and practice; to demands for recognition and general self-assertion by the victims of the old order – the claims of individuals, classes, submerged nations, races, minorities; democratic revolt against the very notion that human beings should (whether or not they can) be moulded by paternalist or any other authoritarian groups; violent rejection of the notion that men should be manufactured like bricks for social structures designed by, or for the benefit of, some privileged group or leader; the desire for the breaking of chains and throwing off of burdens which inspires every revolution in some degree, and militates against the *élitist* notion that societies or states are works of art to be shaped by statesmen – leaders – a class or group of master minds. This is one trend. On the other hand, the very same forces, both scientific and social, make for rational organization; for the rationalization of production, distribution, consumption; and consequently for concentration of power and centralization as the most effective method of getting things done. And this, as the early socialists all too clearly foresaw, leads to the creation of new hierarchies of technical experts, 'engineers of human souls', deliberate creators and moulders of the 'new man', the emergence of the *Massenmensch* – of the reduction of men to 'human material'; to the 'life of the anthill', with all its, by now, notorious consequences of the mechanization, alienation, dehumanization, of entire societies, manipulated by hidden (and sometimes not so hidden) persuaders, of technocratic despotism. And as a result of this, a reaction inevitably follows – various forms of passionate protest, pleas for return to a more human life, to 'organic' society, *Gemeinschaft*; sometimes fed by backward-looking fantasies, at other times fired with dynamic nationalist or racist passion equally menacing to individual liberty or the free use of the imagination and the critical faculties. Or again, the reaction may take the form of indignant defence of menaced individual values, or of a romantic rebellion against 'the machine' or 'the system', by anarchists, students, artists, men in revolt not disciplined by knowledge who wish to opt out of conventional social life or any ordered existence – beatniks, hippies, flower children, irrationalist radicals, terrorists, devotees of the use of purifying violence against a corrupt society, or alternatively of total rejection of power; or yet again, by various Marxist and quasi-Marxist oppositions (most of all in their 'revisionist' or 'humanist' forms).

But if men are to be enabled to control their lives in the light of knowledge of what it is that they are dealing with, and not simply to regard disturbing changes of this kind with mere bewilderment, or fatalistic resignation, or fanaticism, or the disdain of the elect, or a self-destructive desire to surrender to the irresistible, it is desirable that the young, in particular, should be furnished with weapons against such helplessness. They should be given sufficient knowledge both of the genesis of the new order which is rising, and of its character; and since a dominant element in this order is constituted by the vast, swift progress of the natural sciences, and of the consequences, intended and unintended, of simultaneous advances on scientific and technological fronts, they must acquire some understanding of it if they are to exercise a degree of conscious control over it. These may be social issues, and the sociology of the role of the sciences in human lives may seem remote from, say, questions which preoccupy theoretical physicists. But the vast amount of ignorance about what technology is, about its relation to pure research, about the degree to which its methods transform men including scientists, and finally what is common and what is not, to scientific, and literary, and critical or historical thought, is so great (and growing), that this alone puts both statesmen and the elected representatives of the people, and the electorate itself, at the mercy of experts, who are often themselves at best one-eyed. This situation breeds systematic misunderstanding, and leads to the accumulation of power by the experts – scientific middlemen – whom the awe of both public and politicians renders relatively immune to democratic control. It is absurd to regard this state of affairs as irremediable. The irresistible, as Justice Brandeis once observed, is often simply that which is not resisted. This may seem a merely utilitarian reason for the studies advocated in this book, but it is nevertheless a crucial one for mankind at large. If to it are added the claims of disinterested intellectual satisfaction, and the exhilarating prospect of understanding the forces at work in one's world, it offers, to say the very least, sufficient reason for supposing that the enterprise advocated in this book is worth attempting.

Where are we to begin? Merely to preach, merely to encourage scientists to study history or sociology or philosophy, or the great works of man – the classics of literature and art; or (as has been suggested often enough) simply to encourage students of literature or sociology to grasp the methods and the goals of molecular biologists or solid state physicists, this seems plainly useless. Useless, because it does not work. Natural scientists may be bored by, or have no time for, Homer or Michelangelo (even if some among them, not nearly as few as is commonly supposed, were and are highly civilized human beings). Historians and students of literature find it difficult to understand expositions of scientific disciplines. What can be done is something different. To assist scientists or mathematicians towards some understanding of how historians or critics arrive at their judgements (which involves an uncertain but indispensable type of imaginative insight), and how they justify them (an exercise in logic, although at times an unorthodox kind of logic), however it is done, is at once more feasible and far more intellectually valuable than an attempt to 'civilize' a chemist by dwelling on the properties of *The Divine Comedy*, or of the ceiling of the Sistine Chapel, or of the *Agamemnon*, or to try to talk a Greek scholar into taking a canter past the principal landmarks of elementary physiology or theory of numbers. The problem is one of grasp of mental processes, what Whitehead correctly calls adventures of ideas, not of throwing up hastily constructed bridges between 'cultures'. If this task is to be performed, it can be accomplished not by precept but only by example – by the discovery or training of teachers of sufficient knowledge, imagination and talent to make the student see what they see: an experience which, as anyone knows who has ever had a good teacher of any subject, is always fascinating; and can be transforming.

How, it may be asked, is this to be achieved? By what educational reform? The notion that the picture of the world had changed, and that education must change with it, presented itself dramatically to the first advocates of 'modern education' and led to excesses which hold lessons for reformers. In the eighteenth century more than one *philosophe* urged radical reform of education in the direction of reason and enlightenment. The study of dead languages, of history (save as a collection of cautionary examples of the follies, crimes and failures of mankind), of the field of the humanities in general, must be discontinued forthwith, and the new instruments for the discovery of the truth – natural sciences (including the social ones from which much was expected), and the inculcation of civic principles of a utilitarian kind, must immediately be substituted. This, for example, was the programme of conscientious French reformers, Helvétius and his friends, and to some degree of Condorcet. This unhistorical radical positivism, understandable enough during the *ancien régime* in France (or indeed in Germany, Italy or Spain), provoked a violent reaction on the part of the insulted human spirit, of the neglected life of the imagination. This led to the Romantic rebellion; a return to the study of the past, the remote, the peculiar, the irrational, the uncharacteristic; to the rejection of systems, generalization, symmetry, timeless serenity, rationality itself; to the cult of eccentricity and ugliness, as expressions of the revolt of the passions against the 'cold' classifications and abstractions practised by the natural sciences. The *lumières* were accused of spreading darkness: of closing the mind to insight into the inner life and of promoting the atrophy of the will and the emotions, and thereby philistine attitudes to the great masterpieces of art and thought and religious feeling. It is, in part, this nineteenth-century war between the advocates of the humanities and of the sciences, in which intransigent positions were taken, that led finally to a situation which can only be called neither peace nor war – something like a condition of armed neutrality between scientific and humane studies, with an ever widening gulf between them, which it is the business of modern education, if not to abolish, at least to narrow.

Can this be done? It was I think Tolstoy who once observed that what a man perceives clearly – really clearly – he is able to expound simply: and that what is clearly understood (even, I suppose, if it is false) can therefore be communicated by a teacher to a pupil of average responsiveness. He believed that allegations of the impossibility, or acute difficulty, of communicating the technical details of a discipline to untrained minds (not that he thought this particularly important in comparison with central moral truths – the grasp of the real ends of life – but this is not relevant here) were, as often as not, due to the fact that the teacher sought to conceal from himself that he did not begin to see the wood for the trees. Tolstoy was convinced that the salient features of any problem can always be conveyed; and that pleas of difficulty, although sometimes well founded, too often disguised the mentor's own intellectual confusions and insecurity. This, as so much in Tolstoy, may be vastly oversimplified; but again as so often in the ideas of this devastating thinker, it expresses a disagreeable truth. If even a few serious and imaginative teachers with a knack for clear exposition tried to convey what they knew to students on the other side of the barrier, and persisted until they obtained a response, he could not believe that the results would be disappointing. And in this, I strongly suspect, he was right.

FOREWORD

Pretentious rhetoric, deliberate or compulsive obscurity or vagueness, metaphysical patter studded with irrelevant or misleading allusions to (at best) half understood scientific or philosophical theories or to famous names, is an old, but at present particularly prevalent, device for concealing poverty of thought or muddle, and sometimes perilously near a confidence trick. Nevertheless, the increasing effort to drag in scientific notions into the realms of art or ideology, or literary ones into those of the sciences, is itself a pathetic symptom of the craving to bridge a gulf. Impostors, both literary and scientific, or poorly equipped popularizers offer counterfeit commodities because there is a mounting demand for the genuine article, and their shameful activities are as good an index as any to what many in their societies need and search for as best they can. The proposition that education cannot help, that good money cannot drive out bad, seems to me defeatist nonsense: the history of thought from the Greeks onwards testifies against it.

Everyone knows what effect even the informal casual talk of a gifted, enthusiastic and sympathetic schoolmaster can have upon his pupils, both for better and for worse. A capacity for discovery and invention, for basic research and original work, is not always allied to either a desire or a gift for teaching. But sometimes it is. At other times it is the middlemen – those who understand something and tell others, as Voltaire did with his not very perfect exposition of Newton, or, as a century and a half later, those other great *vulgarisiteurs*, Jules Verne and H. G. Wells, did in their own highly imaginative way – that have had an immensely liberating effect. There is no reason why this kind of exposition should not be integrated into academic disciplines, without woolliness, or dilution, or superficiality, or degradation of learning; provided that those who are engaged in it are themselves of sufficient intellectual calibre, and believe in their task, and do not regard it as a chore and a bore to be performed only as an obligation to the age and society in which they live, as a peripheral and undignified labour involving a loss of time that might otherwise be dedicated to their own original work.

I do not mean to imply that a gift for exposition is as valuable as capacity for original thought, still less that all academic disciplines are of equal intrinsic or pedagogical worth. To maintain that they are, is a vulgar educational egalitarianism which does violence to the truth and harm to educational practice. A gifted expositor can put life into virtually any topic: nevertheless there are indices of intellectual power. The academic value of a subject seems to me to depend largely on the ratio of ideas to facts in it. 'Interplay' would doubtless be a better word than 'ratio' to indicate the relationship; nevertheless the latter brings out more clearly the danger of underrating the component of ideas, whether intuitive, empirical or logical (i.e. deductive, hypothetical-deductive, inductive, etc.). Thus, in subjects where the factual component is virtually non-existent, e.g. in logic or pure mathematics, expertise infallibly connotes a high degree of intellectual power. Whatever may be thought of the value of these disciplines, it is plain that only a very gifted man can be a good pure mathematician or a good logician. It could be argued that an accurate account of the rise and fall of export figures for Danish cheeses during a given decade of the nineteenth century might offer material useful to an economic historian capable of valuable original work in his field, or function as an illustration for some new and revolutionary technique for estimating economic change. Consequently the labours of the expert on the sales of Danish cheese might well be more socially useful than an elaborate topological fantasy. Nevertheless our respect for the specialist on cheeses is not high; we value his work but not him; and the sole reason for this is the low content of ideas – hypotheses, powers of reasoning, capacity for general ideas, awareness of the relationship of elements in a total pattern, etc. – in such painstaking but intellectually undemanding work. If the interplay of ideas and facts in subjects so disparate as, say, economic history and theoretical chemistry as a branch of applied

FOREWORD

mathematics, or in social psychology and metallurgy, could be compared by someone who knew one of these subjects well and professionally, and the other through the illumination obtained from a good teacher, this alone would be an enormous source of intellectual exhilaration and profit: it would make a student of this type not only feel, but be, far more at home in the intellectual world of his time. It is the capacity for rising to a clear perception of structures of thought and knowledge, of their similarities and differences, of their methods of discovery and invention and their criteria of truth or validity; above all a grasp of their central principles – and therefore of what is the nerve and muscle and what the surrounding tissue in any human construction, what is novel and revolutionary in a discovery and what is development of existing knowledge – that lifts men intellectually. It is this that elevates them to that power of contemplating patterns, whether permanent or changing, buried in, or imposed on, the welter of experience, which philosophers have regarded as man's highest attribute; but even if they are mistaken in this, it is surely not an unworthy goal for what we like to call higher education.

English

REUBEN BROWER

PREFATORY NOTE[1]

THIS essay was written in response to two main concerns, one common to school and university teachers in the United States and in Great Britain, the other more peculiar to teachers in the States, where experiments in General Education have been going on for more than half a century. The first – the growth in numbers and the decline in ability and taste of readers – was dramatically illustrated years ago in I. A. Richard's *Practical Criticism* and in Q. D. Leavis's *Fiction and the Reading Public*. Increased awareness that 'something was wrong' in the classroom, and more generally, in literary culture beyond the classroom, has led to a new emphasis in schools and universities on 'practical criticism' and 'close reading'. The uncommon common reader and the literary critic of the present generation will have little difficulty in agreeing that the first obligation for both is to confront the work of literature in all its particularity and life. They will also agree, we may assume, that to 'confront' means to respond to particular uses of language – not 'to begin with' or 'at some point', but continuously and alertly – the final purpose being to interpret the work as a *total* expression. Whatever the ultimate question reader or critic may be trying to answer, whether moral or

---

1. This essay, under the title *Reading in Slow Motion*, was originally published in *Reading for Life: Developing the College Student's Lifetime Reading Interest*, edited by Jacob M. Price (Ann Arbor: University of Michigan Press, 1959), copyright by the University of Michigan, and is printed here in a revised version with the permission of the publisher.

aesthetic, historical or sociological, linguistic or psychological, any answer will be valid only in so far as it is based on relevant, disciplined response to the writer's words and to the larger order of experience they shape and create.

The second concern is closely related to the first, since the increase in the size of the reading public is one aspect of 'mass culture' and since mass education has in turn been developed with the aim of giving greater numbers the kind of educational experience once enjoyed only by a minority. The other side of the story needs no retelling here: as more and more people are being educated badly, a new minority – not the older aristocratic few – has been reaching a level of specialization never before equalled. In the United States, where response to an educational need is often more quick than considered (think of the evangelical rush to the 'new mathematics' after Sputnik), there has been a series of attempts to meet the defects of both kinds of education, mass and specialized, by introducing programmes in General Education. Some of the ills of these well-intended experiments have, in this writer's opinion, arisen from a confusion of 'mass' with 'general', from an unacknowledged tendency to create courses of study that are good enough for those who cannot do better. One odd result has followed: the intelligent specialist who is required to take these courses[2] is bored, insulted and dejected by a programme originally designed to enrich his limited specialized diet. Meantime the hungry masses look up and are fed – on diluted 'culture'.

The concern, however, is not with the cultural symptoms that have led to experiments in General Education, but with the quality of the courses that have been invented to cure the disease. Courses in the humanities – a term often used to embrace literature, philosophy, the fine arts and history –

2. In the United States undergraduates are required to take a specified number of courses for a degree. (Honours students are required in addition to do special tutorial work, to write a thesis, and to take a set of examinations on the whole field.) A year 'course' consists ordinarily of a series of classes or formal lectures, with various tests, including a mid-year and a final examination. Grades in courses become a part of the student's permanent record.

have been introduced in many colleges and universities with the aim of introducing students to monuments of Western culture. The typical humanities course in literature is modelled – though with many local variations – on famous originals at Columbia or Chicago. The usual list of books, sometimes read in their entirety, sometimes in selections, will almost invariably include the Bible and works of Homer, Plato, Shakespeare, Dante, seasoned with 'moderns' from Montaigne to Goethe and Camus. Many, often the majority of the authors, are read in translation, and the emphasis in such courses tends to be on Great ideas or attitudes, or more vaguely, on the Western Tradition. 'General' as used in this context has acquired resounding connotations of universal, true and timeless. The comic – or tragic – climax of this version of General Education has been reached in the *Syntopicon* published by the Encyclopaedia Britannica and the University of Chicago, in which one finds alphabetically arranged, the leading ideas of the Great Books, with citation of texts where each idea is treated. The temptation to teacher and student to short-cut the book itself, to reduce great and complex expressions to easily portable lessons and truths, is enormous.

The following essay offers the suggestion that there is more than one way of defining 'general' in a General Education course in the humanities. What, for example, could be more general than basic training in reading and in discrimination? Although no one in his right mind would be 'against' Great Books, it may be agreed that more important than familiarity with a set of canonical texts is the power to read a Great Book on one's own and to read it well. The final aim of General Education in the humanities is not to invent monumental programmes, but to ensure the continuing life of a public for 'high' literature.

*

The question put to me at a conference[3] on undergraduate

3. The description of an imaginary course later in the text is based on courses given at Amherst College and Harvard University. The

education, 'How shall we encourage and influence the lifetime reading habit?' brought to mind the words of Solon that Croesus recalled on the funeral pyre: 'I shall not call you fortunate until I learn that the end of your life was happy too.' Call no student a lifetime reader until... No teacher can be quite sure that he has a lifetime habit of reading, and if asked whether his students have acquired it or formed good reading habits, he will probably feel most uneasy about making an answer. But assuming that we could see each student's life as a whole, *sub specie aeternitatis*, we should have to ask the further question: What reading habit are we evaluating? In the age of the New Stupid (a term Aldous Huxley once used for the age of mass literacy), nearly everyone has a reading habit of some sort. Everyone runs through the morning newspaper or *Time* and *Life* strictly as a matter of daily or weekly routine. Each social group has its 'great readers', a term of admiration used to cover a wide range of activities that have little more than the printed page in common. There is, for example, reading as anodyne, and reading as extended daydream. There is reading as pursuit of fact or of useful technical know-how, and reading that may or may not be useful, when we are interested solely in understanding a theory or a point of view. Still more remote from immediate usefulness comes reading as active amusement, a game demanding the highest alertness and the finest degree of sensibility, 'judgement ever awake and steady self-possession with enthusiasm and feeling profound or vehement'. Reading at this level – to borrow Coleridgean terms a second time – 'brings the whole soul of man into activity'. Coleridge was speaking of the poet and the power of imagination, but his words describe very well the way we read when we enter into, or rather engage in, experiences of imaginative literature. I say 'amusement', not 'pleasure', to stress the play

---

particular exercises and devices described are all drawn from these courses, but all were not used in any one course. My colleagues in both institutions will best know how much I owe to their ingenuity and their cheerful support in making many experiments in slow reading.

of mind, the play of the whole being, that reading of this sort calls for. I am hardly suggesting that literary experience is not a 'good', that it is not in some indirect and profound way morally valuable. But if it is to do us any good, it must be fun. The first line of a poem by D. H. Lawrence offers an appropriate motto for teachers and students of literature:

If it's never any fun, don't do it!

Active 'amusement' is the reading habit I am concerned with here and more especially with the role played by the teacher of literature in encouraging students to acquire it. I prefer to speak of the 'teacher of literature', not the 'humanities', because that noble term has become so debased in current usage, and because teachers of texts in humanities courses are or should be teachers of literature. The teacher of Plato or Hobbes or Hume is not only interpreting a system but an expression, an expression that uses many resources of language and uses them in ways that profoundly influence how we take the writer's radical meaning. We cannot subtract from our interpretations the effect of Platonic comedy or of Hobbesian metaphor or of Hume's dispassionate irony. But it remains true that the teacher of literature in the conventional sense has a special interest in encouraging students to respond actively to all the uses of language, from the barely referential to the rhythmic. He is always more or less consciously urging his students to make themselves readers of imagination.

How will the teacher go about reaching this noble aim? By a method that might be described as 'slow motion', by slowing down the process of reading to observe what is happening, in order to attend very closely to the words, their uses, and their meanings. Since poetry is literature in its essential and purest form – the mode of writing in which we find at the same time the most varied uses of language and the highest degree of order – the first aim of the teacher of literature will be to make his students better readers of poetry. He will try by every means in his power

ENGLISH

to bring out the complete and agile response to words that is demanded by a good poem.

But why a course in slow reading? The parent who has a son or daughter in college[4] may well feel confused, since almost certainly he has at least one child with a reading difficulty, the most common complaint being that the child cannot read fast enough. As the parent himself watches the mounting lists of important books, and as he scans the rivers of print in the daily paper, he may well feel that like Alice and the Red Queen, he and his children are going faster and faster but getting nowhere.

The difficulties of parent and child point to conditions that have led to the introduction of how-to-read courses in our colleges and universities. We might note first the sheer mass of printed material to which we are exposed – not to mention the flood of words and images pouring through radio and television. If by temperament or principle we resist the distracting appeals of the press and other media, we must nevertheless read a great deal as we run if we are to perform our tasks as citizens and wage-earners. Add to such facts the changes in family life that have altered reading habits of both parents and children. Memorization of Bible texts and poetry is hardly common in school or home, and the family reading circle where books were read aloud and slowly, has all but disappeared even from the idyllic backwaters of academic communities. Yet many if not all of the writers of the past, from Homer to novelists like Jane Austen and Dickens, have assumed reading aloud and a relatively slow rate of intellectual digestion. Literature of the first order calls for lively reading; we must almost act it out as if we were taking parts in a play. As the average high school[5] student reads more and more with less and less wholeness of attention, he may become positively incapaci-

4. In American usage, a college is an institution of higher learning at the university level. The typical liberal arts college might be compared to an Oxbridge college set up and run independently, apart from a university.

5. A publicly maintained free school, where students may be prepared for college and university.

tated for reading the classics or any literature on his own. Incidentally, the parent of the slow reader should take heart: his child may not be stupid, but more than ordinarily sensitive to words. He may in fact have the makings of a poet.

Another change in pre-college education is almost certainly connected with the decline in the ability to read literature of the first quality, a change that points also to profound changes in the literary public of the past century and a half. Until thirty or forty years ago a high proportion of students of literature in our liberal arts colleges had received a considerable training in Latin or Greek. If we move back to the much smaller reading publics of the seventeenth and eighteenth centuries, the audiences for whom much of our greatest literature was written, the relative number of readers trained in the classics becomes much higher. The principal method of teaching the ancient languages, translation into English or from English into Latin or Greek, may have had disadvantages compared with the direct method of today, but as a basic preparation for the study of literature it can hardly be surpassed. It may be doubted whether learning of a foreign language can take place without some translation, at least into what experts in linguistics call the 'meta-language' of the learner. To translate from Latin and Greek demanded close attention to the printed word, and since the ideas being communicated and the linguistic and literary forms through which they were expressed were often quite unlike those in English, translation compelled the closest scrutiny of meanings and forms of expression in both the ancient and the modern language. Although the old-time classicist may not always have been successful as a teacher of literature, he cannot often be accused of lacking rigour. His students had to spend a good many hours in school and college reading some pieces of literature very attentively. One purpose of a course in slow reading is to offer a larger number of present-day undergraduates an equivalent for the older classical training in interpretation of texts.

It might be noted that Coleridge, who harshly criticized the practice of Latin verse-making in English schools, paid the highest tribute to that 'severe master, the Reverend James Bowyer':

At the same time that we were studying the Greek tragic poets, he made us read Shakespeare and Milton as lessons: and they were the lessons too, which required the most time and trouble to *bring up*, so as to escape his censure. I learned from him, that poetry, even that of the loftiest and, seemingly, that of the wildest odes, had a logic of its own, as severe as that of science; and more difficult, because more subtle, more complex, and dependent on more and more fugitive causes. In the truly great poets, he would say, there is a reason assignable not only for every word, but for the position of every word; and I well remember that, availing himself of the synonymes to the Homer of Didymus, he made us attempt to show, with regard to each, why it would not have answered the same purpose; and wherein consisted the peculiar fitness of the word in the original text.

In our own English compositions (at least for the last three years of our school education) he showed no mercy to phrase, metaphor, or image, unsupported by a sound sense, or where the same sense might have been conveyed with equal force and dignity in plainer words. *Lute*, *harp*, and *lyre*, *Muse*, *Muses*, and *inspirations*, *Pegasus*, *Parnassus*, and *Hippocrene* were all an abomination to him. In fancy I can almost hear him now, exclaiming: 'Harp? Harp? Lyre? Pen and ink, boy, you mean! Muse, boy, Muse? Your nurse's daughter, you mean! Pierian spring? Oh aye! the cloister-pump, I suppose!'

The Reverend James Bowyer and not Coleridge, it appears, was the original New Critic, which is to say that much New Criticism is old criticism writ large. Bowyer's example suggests another important point to which I shall return: that teaching of reading is necessarily teaching of writing. The student cannot show his teacher or himself that he has had an important and relevant literary experience except in writing or in speaking that is as disciplined as good writing.

To teach reading or any other subject in the style of the Reverend Bowyer demands an attitude towards the job that is obvious but easily overlooked in our larger universities, where increasing numbers of students often impose mass production methods. The most important requirement for teaching an undergraduate course – beyond belief in what one is doing – is to keep this question in mind: What is happening to the student? Other questions soon follow: What do I want him to do and how can I get him to do it? Planning and teaching from this point of view makes the difference between a course that engages the student and one that merely displays the teacher. The perfect model for the teacher of literature as for the teacher of science is Agassiz, who would come into the laboratory, pour out a basket of bones before the student, and leave him alone to sort them out. After this introduction to the 'material' of the course, Agassiz limited his teaching to infrequent visits, when he checked on the learner's progress by an occasional nod or shake of the head to say 'That's right!' or 'No, not that!' The great thing in teaching is to get the basket of bones before the student and get him to sorting them for himself as soon as possible. What we must avoid at all costs is sorting out all the bones in advance. Agassiz's principle is of great importance in the teaching of literature, where far too often we present the undergraduate with the end-products of literary scholarship without being sure he has read or has the capacity of reading the works we are interpreting.

If we are interested in fostering a habit of reading well, we must set up our introductory courses on a principle very different from that underlying the older survey[6] or the now more fashionable history-of-ideas course.[7] We are not handing the student a body of knowledge, so much 'material' – the history of the Romantic Movement or an anatomy of the concepts labelled 'Romanticism' – however useful such knowledge may be at a later stage in literary education.

---

6. Usually an introductory course dealing with the whole field, in chronological order, e.g. 'English Literature, from Beowulf to T. S. Eliot'.

7. See Prefatory Note, page 3.

Our aim rather is to get the student in a position where he can learn for himself. If we succeed, we have reason to believe that he may acquire a lifetime habit of learning independently. The teacher who is working towards this noble end will always be working *with* the student, not *for* him or *over* him. Whitehead used to say that the student should feel he is present while the teacher is thinking, present at an occasion when thought is in process. Those who knew Whitehead in the classroom will know what he meant and why he never seemed to be lecturing, even before a class of a hundred or two hundred students. His listeners never knew exactly where he was coming out. Not knowing where one is coming out is an essential part of the experience of thinking.

To get the student to a point where he can learn for himself requires therefore a redefinition of a 'lecture'. It asks the teacher to share his ignorance with his students as well as his knowledge. Or if professors shrink from admitting less than omniscience, it calls for at least a Socratic simulation of ignorance. What is wanted is the 'nonlecture', to borrow E. E. Cummings's happy term, an action performed by the teacher but clearly directed to the next performance of the student. The ideal nonlecturer is setting a job for the student and showing him how he would go about doing it. If he is not in fact setting a job, he will clearly indicate a relevant kind of job to be done. A proper job means setting a question and offering a way, not a formula, for answering it. Student and teacher must clearly understand that a course in interpretation is a course in 'right answering', not a course in 'right answers'.

But in order not to create a wrong impression, a word needs to be said here about method, a term liable to please some and displease others for equally bad reasons. There is certainly no single sacred technique for teaching reading at the level I have in mind. In teaching literature – unlike science, one may suppose – no holds are barred, providing they work and providing that the injury to the work and to the student does not exceed the limits of humanity. The most distinctive feature of the kind of literature course I am about to describe is that the teacher does have some 'holds', some ways of reading that he is willing to demonstrate and that his students can imitate. In this respect 'Literature X',[8] as I shall call it, differs from the old-time appreciation course in which the teacher mounted the platform and sang a rhapsody which he alone was capable of understanding and which the student memorized, with the usual inaccuracies, for the coming examination.

Let me now attempt to describe Literature X, a course in slow reading that aims to meet the general requirements I have been outlining and that is designed also to meet the needs of young readers in our colleges and universities. I have said that we want students to increase their power of engaging in imaginative experience, and we assume – this was implied by our earlier reference to Coleridge – that a work of literature offers us an experience through words that is different from average, everyday experience. It is different in its mysterious wholeness, in the number of elements embraced and in the variety and closeness of their relationship. When Othello, just before Desdemona's death, says, 'Put out the light, and then put out the light', we feel not only the horror of his intention but also a remarkable concentration of much that has gone on before: the moving history of the relations between the lovers and between them and Iago, the echoed presence of earlier moments of 'lightness' and 'darkness'.

We all agree that such experiences in literature are wonderful, but what can a teacher do to guide a student to discover them? He will of course start from his own excitement, and he will do everything he can to infect his students with it: he will try to express in other words what Othello and the audience are experiencing; he will read the passage aloud or get a student to do it; he will exhort and entreat. But finally he cannot hand over his feelings to his students; he cannot force them to be more sensitive than they are. What can he do that the students may also do and

8. Each separate course (see note 2, page 2) has a number.

that they can imitate when they read another scene or another play? He can do a great deal if he remembers that while he and his students do not have a common nervous system, they do have the same printed page and they share some knowledge of the English language. He will therefore direct their attention to the words, to what they mean and to their connexion with other words and meanings. In considering the 'put out the light' speech from *Othello*, the teacher may begin by asking what the words mean in terms of stage business. He may then call for a paraphrase: for 'put out the light' someone may offer 'bring darkness', or 'put an end to'. The class can next be asked to connect this expression with others used elsewhere in the play. Someone may recall Othello's earlier line associating Desdemona with darkness and death: '. . . *when I love thee not,/Chaos is come again.*' The reader can now begin to appreciate the poignancy and the irony of Othello's picturing his action as 'putting out the light'. So by directing attention to words, their meanings, and relationships, the teacher may put his students in a position where they too will feel the pity and terror of this moment in the play.

We might describe Literature X as a 'mutual demonstration society', the work of the course being carried on mainly through student–teacher explorations of the kind I have been attempting to illustrate. For the students the most important and most strenuous demonstrations will be the exercises[9] that they write on their own after being suitably prepared by the teacher. *Othello* may serve as an example once more. After several classes of reading aloud and exploring connexions in the earlier acts of the play, an exercise will be set on a speech or scene from the last act. The students now have an opportunity to show whether they can practise independently the sort of interpretation they have been attempting in class. To guide them, they will be given an exercise sheet with a very carefully planned series of questions. Beginning with queries on words and phrases, the exercise goes on to ask about relationships of

9. A sample exercise is given in the Appendix.

various kinds, and it concludes with a question demanding a generalization about the work as a whole or about a type of literature or experience. An exercise on *Othello* might finally call for a statement about the nature of Othello's tragedy and for a tentative definition of 'tragic' as used in Shakespearean drama. But the words 'tragic' or 'tragedy' will not necessarily appear in the directions; rather, the students will be impelled to talk about these concepts because they are relevant. In the class on the exercise papers the student and his teacher will be admirably prepared to consider what is meant by tragic literature and experience. These discussions of the exercises should be among the most valuable classes in the course. Here the student can learn by comparing where he succeeded or failed as an interpreter, and frequently he may have the pleasure of finding that he has taught his teacher something, an event that can give satisfaction to both parties and that can take place more often in a course where the student is an active participant, not a passive member of an audience.

Literature X as a whole will consist of a series of these exercise waves, with some more terrifying than others, the seventh and last coming when the students are given two or more weeks without classes in which to read new material – poems, plays, or novels – with no teacher to guide them.

The course will not begin with Shakespeare, although Shakespeare is the necessary measure of imaginative experience and of the capacity to engage in it. We shall begin rather with the smaller model of the short poem, because as I have said it offers literary experience in its purest form. By beginning with poems we can be reasonably sure that the student learns early to distinguish between life and literature and not to be unduly distracted by questions of biography and history or by social and psychological problems of the type raised so often by the novel. Most important, the student will learn at the outset to deal with *wholes*, since within the limits of a class hour or a brief paper he can arrive at an interpretation of a whole literary expression. Poems may come to stand in his mind as Platonic forms of true and complete literary experience.

Beginning with poems has another advantage if students are to learn the value of attending closely to language and if they are to see the satisfactions that come from alert and accurate reading. In the small world of a sonnet, a reader can see how a single word may cause a shift in the equilibrium of feeling in the whole poem. So when Shakespeare says:

> *For thy sweet love remember'd such wealth brings*
> *That then I scorn to change my state with kings.*

'state' carries connotations of Elizabethan *state*, and as a result the speaker's voice takes on a tone of grandeur, a somewhat stagey grandeur that reminds us of gestures in a play. But the word 'state' would hardly impart that quality without the reference to 'kings'. This fairly simple example brings home the importance in interpretation of considering the context. A course in interpretation is a course in definition by context, in seeing how words are given rich and precise meaning through their interrelations with other words. The student who acquires this habit of definition will be a better reader of philosophy or law or any other type of specialized discourse, and he may learn something about the art of writing, of how to control context in order to express oneself.

Reading poems also offers one of the best ways of lifting the student from adolescent to adult appreciation of literature. The adult reader realizes that reading a work of literature is at once a solitary and a social act. In reading we are alone, but we are also among the company of readers assumed by the poem or play or novel. The poem is more than a personal message, it invites us to move out of ourselves, to get into an 'act', to be another self in a fictive drama. The sonnet of Shakespeare we have just quoted seems to call for a very simple identification of the actual reader with the imagined speaker,

> *When in disgrace with fortune and men's eyes*
> *I all alone beweep my outcast state . . .*

(Many will recall their own youthful readings of the poem.) Yet even this simple if not sentimental sonnet asks something more of us in the end; it asks us to take on the demonstrative air of the theatrical lover, to protest in language we would never actually use in our most romantic moments.

In Literature X we shall start by reading poems, and start with no apparent method or at least with method well concealed. We begin, as Frost says, with delight, to end in wisdom. 'What is it *like*,' we say rather crudely, 'to read this poem?' 'With what feeling are we left at its close?' 'What sort of person is speaking?' 'What is he *like*, and where does he reveal himself most clearly?' 'In what line or phrase?' We may then ask if there is a key phrase or word in the poem, and we can begin to introduce the notion of the poem as a structure, as an ordered experience built up through various kinds of meaning controlled in turn by various uses of language.

Remembering our questions about the speaker, we first direct attention to dramatic uses of language, to the ways in which the words create a character speaking in a certain role. We may ask, for example, who is speaking in Keats's sonnet on Chapman's *Homer*. An alert student may point out that he is a traveller (many do not see this), and that he uses idioms with a medieval colouring: 'realms', 'goodly', 'bards in fealty', 'demesne'. But the speaker does not continue to talk in this vein:

Till I heard Chapman speak out loud and bold.

He has changed, and the drama moves into a second act. We hear a voice that is powerful and young, the voice of the New World discoverer and the Renaissance astronomer. We now point out to our young reader (if he is still listening) that the poem is indeed an 'act'. The poet is speaking *as if* he were a traveller-explorer, and the whole poem is built on a metaphor. So, while reading many poems, we may introduce a few basic notions of literary design and some useful critical terms. But our emphasis will always be on the term as a tool, as a device for calling attention to the poem and how it is made. In time we can turn to study of the poem as an experience of ordered sounds, but not, we hasten to add, of sounds divorced from sense. Our aim in talking about rhythmic pattern, as in considering dramatic and metaphorical design, is to show how the poem 'works' and what it expresses. We see, for example, that as Keats's sonnet moves from the medieval to the modern speaker, and as the metaphor also shifts, the rhythm changes from the 'broken' couplets and inversions of the octave to the long and steady sweep of the sestet. The whole sonnet in its beautiful interaction of parts gives us the sense of discovery and release into a new world of literary and aesthetic experience.

Following a period of reading poems, the course will move ahead to a play by Shakespeare so that students can see at once that the way in which they have read poems works also for a poetic drama and that there are some basic similarities between the structure of these different types of literature. They may see, for example, that the man speaking in a poem corresponds to the character in a play, that Shakespeare has his large metaphors just as Keats has his smaller ones.

From drama we go to the reading of a novel, often via short stories. The short story like the poem gives us literary experience in microcosm and makes it easier to see analogies between fiction and poetry, to see that a tale by Hawthorne is the unfolding of a single metaphorical vision, or that the narrator in a story by Joyce controls our sense of being within the child's world, exiled from adult society. The novel, especially as we have it in its classic nineteenth-century form, in Dickens or George Eliot, demands a very different reading from a Shakespearean drama, but by putting the same questions to both genres their likeness and their unlikeness can be defined, and the exact quality of a particular work can be discovered. The student will find, for example, that the 'marshes' and 'mists' of *Great Expectations* are nearer to the fixed symbols of allegory than to the fluid metaphors of Shakespeare. But he can also see that in a novel as in a poem the narrative voice is of immense importance. Comparison of the opening scene in the film of *Great Expectations* with Dickens's telling shows that when the sanely humorous, entertaining voice of Dickens is removed, we are left with images of pure nightmare. The major themes of *Great Expectations*, guilt and innocence, justice and injustice, are not un-Shakespearean, but we can hardly read the novel without an awareness that unlike *King Lear* and *Macbeth* and like most novels, the imaginative world of *Great Expectations* has a date. Jaggers is an awesome symbol of the link between criminality and legal justice, but he also embodies a sharp criticism of the actual court and prison world of mid-nineteenth-century England.

Reading a novel forcibly reminds us that literature is embedded in history, that the meaning of the work in itself changes when we view it in relation to other works and to the social situation in which it first appeared. Literature X will move on in its later phases to some experiments in historical interpretation, 'historical' being used here to include the relation of a work to its time, especially to more or less contemporary works, and to literary tradition. If we return to *Othello* or *Coriolanus* after reading the *Iliad* and after gaining some familiarity with the heroic tradition in Renaissance epic and drama, we find that both plays are clearer and richer in their meaning. We see in *Coriolanus* what happens when an Achilles enters the Roman forum: the simple absolutes of the hero, the code that makes Coriolanus prefer a 'noble life before a long' one, bring confusion in a civil society. The teacher of our ideal course will not merely lay a comparison of this sort before his students, he will try to get them into a position where they can make the comparison for themselves. He will use all the ingenuity he can muster to devise assignments in which the student can practise thinking historically about works of literature.

In a year in which the class has made some study of the hero in Homer and in the Renaissance, a project might be focused on Fielding's *Tom Jones*. While the students are reading the novel outside class (it takes time!), they would study with their teacher readings useful for interpreting the novel in relation to the heroic tradition and to the climate of moral opinion in the eighteenth century. They could observe in Dryden's *Mac Flecknoe* the shift from the Renaissance 'heroick' to the mock-heroic, and in *The Rape of the Lock* they could see how allusions to the ancient heroic world are used to satirize eighteenth-century high society while giving the world of the poem splendour and moral seriousness. After comparing the mock-heroic in Pope and Fielding, they might attempt a definition of the hero in *Tom Jones*. By skilful prodding (in an exercise) they could be led to see that Fielding has created a new type of hero, a youth who is at once ridiculous and charmingly 'good-natured', that although he finally gains a modicum of 'prudence', he wins his way largely through 'benevolence' and 'goodness of heart'.

As a final step in this experiment, there might be a series of readings in Chesterfield, Hume and Dr Johnson, all concerned with social 'goodness', and more especially with 'prudence' and 'benevolence'. The students would then be asked to define and place the moral attitudes expressed in *Tom Jones*, through comparing them with similar attitudes expressed in these eighteenth-century moralists. By projects of this type undergraduates could be given some practice – at an elementary level – in writing intellectual history. At the same time their earlier practice in interpretation would protect them from reducing the experience of the novel to the abstracted idea. But they would also begin to see that a purely literary judgement is finally impossible, that we are impelled to move back from literature to life. Dr Johnson's famous comparison of Fielding and Richardson might be used to show that 'liking' or 'disliking' a novel is an act of moral evaluation. At the end of Literature X, by returning to poetry we could make the point that a choice between poems is a choice between lives.

You may be asking by now what the connexion is

between our ideal course and the lifetime reading habits of undergraduates. I should reply that Literature X attempts to influence future reading habits by keeping to the principle of student activity. No test or exercise or final examination asks the student to 'give back' the 'material' of the course. On the contrary, each stage of the work is planned with a view to how the student reads the *next* work, whether poem or play or novel. At the end of the first half of the course the student is sent off to read and interpret on his own another play of Shakespeare and another novel. He is given leading questions that impel him to do likewise 'differently'. An appropriate mid-year examination in the course might consist of a sight poem to interpret and an essay-exercise on a longer work read outside class. The test for the second half-year (whether an examination or a long essay) would ordinarily be based on a set of texts to be used in interpreting a work in the manner of the project on *Tom Jones*.

But the teacher of a course in slow reading will always be haunted by the question once asked by a colleague of mine: 'Our students learn *how* to read, but *do* they read?' Do they, for example, ever read an author, read every one of his books they can lay their hands on, with an urge to know the writer's work as a whole? Can we do anything in our ideal course to stimulate this most valuable habit? Some modest experiments can be made, I believe, and with some assurance of success. A model can be set by reading generously in a single poet, preferably a recent one, such as Frost, Yeats or Eliot. Or the teacher can give the class a start by reading a few poems in each of a number of writers, and then send the students off to read one of the poets independently. After some weeks they might write an essay 'On Reading So-and-So'. The essay must have a point (surprisingly few students know what a point is) supported by deft and apt interpretation of particular poems. The novel, the most important form for habitual readers in this generation, presents a problem, since we can hardly read all or even several novels of the same writer within the limits of an introductory course. But two novels and some stories by a single writer may rouse some readers to go ahead on their own, and sometimes the discovery that a difficult writer – James or Joyce – is understandable and rewarding or that an old-fashioned writer – Fielding or Jane Austen – is amusing, will start a student along the right path. The best way to influence later habits is the natural way: recommending without system books we have read with pleasure and without ulterior motives. Students recognize the difference between love and duty, and they will respond to genuine enthusiasm and avoid books that they 'ought to' read or – and this is the lowest of all academic appeals – that 'fill a gap' in preparing for general examinations or graduate school placement tests.

If we turn our attention from lifetime reading habits to the larger educational influence of courses in slow reading, we can note some possible correlations between classroom and later performances. In this connexion we should recall the value for close reading of practice in equally close writing. The student who looks at poems as carefully as we have suggested will understand that poetry begins in grammar and that to express a just appreciation of a poem demands fine control of grammar on the part of the appreciator. But to help the student make such discoveries calls for guidance in small classes or at least careful criticism of written exercises. Good writing is an art not amenable to mass production methods.

Attentive criticism of written work is almost certainly of much more value for teaching good reading and writing than the usual discussions or section[10] meetings. The value of a discussion meeting does not depend primarily on size, as many assume, but on the planning that precedes the meeting and the direction of the conversation to a defined goal. In our course in slow reading the discussion is not an adden-

10. Large lecture courses are often divided into groups of fifteen to twenty members, who meet once or twice a week, in addition to the lecture meeting. Sections are often taught by assistants or young instructors.

dum, but the culminating act towards which the teacher's demonstration and the student's exercise have been directed. Under these conditions student and teacher are fully prepared to say something meaningful to each other, since they have before them well-defined questions to pursue and alternative expressed answers to compare and judge.

But discussion of this type need not be vocal. The student can carry it on internally during a lecture, if the lecture is an exercise in how to ask and answer a question of interpretation. The indispensable requirement for an active course in literature is not 'sections', but some form of independent performance for an attentive critical audience of one. Here is where large-scale production methods break down, and limitations in size are necessary. Very few readers can handle more than twenty to twenty-five papers of the type I have been describing and maintain the necessary vigilance and the power of viewing them as individual performances. A reader[11] can handle them in the usual fashion – grade them and add a complimentary or devastating comment – but he cannot give them critical attention at a high level. The student who is to rise to the kind of reading and writing called for in our ideal course must feel that he has a responsible reader, one who addresses himself to this essay and to this mind. The most valuable discussion a teacher can give is a comment surely directed to an individual written performance. Here we have the ideal section: two actors engaged in a Socratic dialogue. A teacher who is not bewildered and dulled by reading too many papers on the same topic will be able to judge the student's present achievement in relation to what he has done in the past. He can also help him keep track of his development and show him where he is going, and when he has failed, show him how to build on an earlier successful performance. Again Coleridge's Reverend Bowyer may serve as a guide:

... there was one custom of our master's, which I cannot pass over in silence, because I think it imitable and worthy of

11. Or 'grader', an assistant, often a graduate student, who reads and grades papers for the lecturer.

imitation. He would often permit our exercises, under some pretext of want of time, to accumulate, till each had four or five to be looked over. Then placing the whole number abreast on his desk, he would ask the writer, why this or that sentence might not have found as appropriate a place under this or that other thesis: and if no satisfying answer could be returned, and two faults of the same kind were found in one exercise, the irrevocable verdict followed, the exercise was torn up, and another on the same subject to be produced, in addition to the tasks of the day. The reader will, I trust, excuse this tribute of recollection to a man, whose severities, even now, not seldom furnish the dreams, by which the blind fancy would fain interpret to the mind the painful sensations of distempered sleep; but neither lessen nor dim the sense of my moral and intellectual obligations.

The marker of an English paper, as Coleridge realized though with 'painful sensations', is a very important person indeed; he becomes the higher literary conscience, the intellectual guardian angel of his students.

It is evident that education in literature of this kind must be personal, and expensive, though scarcely more expensive than education in the sciences. Let us have at least as generous a supply of readers and conference rooms as we have of laboratory assistants and laboratories. The humanities cannot flourish without *humanitas*. A protest is in order against the inhumanity of the humanities when in some of our larger institutions the study of Great Books[12] is reduced to display lectures before audiences of five and six hundred, and when the individual performance is measured by machine-graded examinations.

The teaching of great literary texts in humanities courses has also had other if less depressing results which the teacher of literature should note if he is to fulfil his proper educational role. Because many works are taught in translation and taught often by staffs including many non-specialists in language and literature, and because the texts are often presented in some broad historical framework, a work of imaginative literature tends to be treated either as a docu-

12. See Prefatory Note, page 3.

ment for studying the history of ideas or as a text for illustrating and enforcing desirable moral and social attitudes. Though neither of these approaches is in itself harmful or inappropriate to a university, it may involve serious losses, especially in courses in which many students are reading for the first time – or for the first time at an adult level – masterpieces of European literature. There is a danger, which is increased by the large amounts of reading assigned in Great Books courses, that rich and special experiences will be too readily reduced to crude examples of a historic idea or a moral principle. Though the reductions may be necessary and useful for certain purposes, we must not let students make them too soon or too easily, not if we are seriously concerned with lifetime habits of reading. The undergraduate who masters the trick too early and too well may in the process suffer real damage. He may have acquired the dubious art of reading carelessly, of making the reduction *before* reading, and he may have lowered rather than increased his capacity for responding precisely to a particular work and for making fine discriminations between works.

Hence the special function of the teacher of literature, which is not to be confused with that of the historian or the moral philosopher. The teacher of literature in a humanities course must feel he has betrayed a trust if he has not given the lay reader what he is best qualified to give: training in the literary disciplines of reading and writing. It is pertinent to recall the historic definition of the humanities as it stands in the *Oxford English Dictionary*: 'Learning or literature concerned with human culture, as grammar, rhetoric, poetry, and especially the ancient Latin and Greek classics.' I suspect that some of the more enthusiastic general educators may be surprised by the words that follow 'human culture': 'as grammar, rhetoric, poetry . . .' (The order of items in the list is instructive, too.) The disciplines named are the ones that the teacher of literature has a special responsibility to impart. He is, like Horace's poet, a guardian of the language who shows (as Pope translates it) 'no mercy to an empty line'. His prime object is to maintain fineness of response to words, and his students rightly assume that he will be adept in discovering and illustrating refinements in writing whether in a great book or a student essay. This guardianship, once performed by teachers of the ancient Latin and Greek classics, now falls to the teachers of English and other modern literatures. Why is this so? Because they are committed to the principle that the study of letters is inseparable from the study of language.

Study of literature based on this principle can hardly be carried on in a course based mainly on texts in translation. Translations have their place in a course in interpretation, but only as ancillary to the main business of close reading in the original. The finer distinctions, the finer relationships which we are training our students to discover and make are almost invariably dulled or lost in the process of translation. We want the student to acquire the habit of recognizing and making such distinctions in his *own* language, and we can hardly teach him to do it if the examples before him are relatively crude. Whitehead once remarked when discussing Plato's cosmology, 'After all, the translators of Plato have had B+ philosophic minds.' With rare exceptions the translators of literature have had literary minds of similar quality. There are of course the handful of translations that are masterpieces, such as Pope's *Iliad*, North's *Plutarch*, and Dryden's *Aeneid*, texts that can bear the close study necessary for literary education. Ironically enough, these are the very translations avoided in most Great Books courses.

In speaking of the necessity for close attention to language I am not forgetting that teachers of literature are also teachers of human culture and that they are therefore guardians of important values. But they do not set out to teach these values, although they inevitably impart them by the way they talk and act in the presence of works of literature. But they are especially concerned with another task, with teaching ways of discovering and experiencing values expressed through literary objects. The most precious thing they can give their students is some increase of power, some help however humble in getting into Shakespeare or Dr Johnson or Joyce.

We may hope that a student who has learned how to get into these writers will go back for further experiences after he has left the classroom and the university. That he surely will we cannot say. Even if he does not return to Shakespeare or Johnson, the experiences in the classroom almost certainly have their value and their effect in determining the quality of his later reading. One play well read with a good teacher and well digested in a reflective essay may serve as a touchstone of what literary experience can be. But finally, our belief that students' habits of reading are permanently affected is Platonic. The model for most cultural education is to be found in the third book of the *Republic*:

... our young men, dwelling as it were in a healthy region, may receive benefit from all things about them; the influence that emanates from works of beauty may waft itself to eye or ear like a breeze that brings health from wholesome places, and so from earliest childhood insensibly guide them to likeness, to friendship, to harmony with beautiful reason.

In the effort to realize this Platonic vision in a modern university the undergraduate library plays a most important role. It is there that we may surround the young with fair works of literature through which they may come into 'harmony with beautiful reason'. No one knows how born readers are produced, but we can put books in their way and in the way of the less happily born in the hope that proximity will have its effect as it does in the formation of more mundane habits. Of one thing I am convinced: that a born reader on a library staff can have a tremendous effect on young readers who come his way. I remember with gratitude two librarians of that description, one in school and one in college, who led us to read books we might never have looked into by sharing their love for what they had read. If I were to found a library dedicated to influencing the reading habit, I should place a half-dozen of these enthusiasts at strategic points to ensnare wandering students. They would not necessarily be trained librarians, and they would surely waste students' time and occasionally disturb their colleagues, but like great authors they would create an ever-widening circle of readers. Mere teachers of literature could hardly hope to compete with them, and might in time quietly disappear from the academic scene.

APPENDIX: FINAL EXERCISE ON *OTHELLO*

I. OBJECT OF EXERCISE. Your object is to explore certain uses of language and a related dramatic pattern in *Othello* and to show what they express.

II. PREPARATION. 1. Read and interpret the speech of Othello, at II, i, 185 ('It gives me wonder great as my content...').
  (a) What attitude of Othello at this moment do these lines express? Note and describe some uses of language by which this mood is projected.
  (b) Notice especially the words

  If it were now to die,
  'Twere now to be most happy...

  What meaning do they have for Othello? What different meaning do they have for a spectator who is aware of the sequel? How would you describe the emotional response which accompanies this perception?

2. Now read and interpret the speech of Othello at V, ii, 1–22.
  (a) What attitude of Othello's at this moment do these lines express? By what uses of language is this attitude projected?
  (b) Consider especially the words

  So sweet was ne'er so fatal. (line 20)

  By these words Othello expresses an evaluation of the situation. How does the spectator's evaluation differ from his? What sort of an emotional response accompanies the perception of this difference?

3. How are these two passages alike? Compare at least one other passage of the play that resembles them.
4. You have now noticed at least three moments of the play in which the spectator's evaluation differs from Othello's. How, because of these differences, *must* a reader view Othello? (If you use terms such as 'tragic' and 'ironic', be sure to indicate what they mean in relation to the passages you discuss.)

III. WRITING. Make use of your explorations and findings in an essay focused on question 4, supporting your points by particular examples from your preparation of 1, 2 (especially), and 3.

History

J. D. HEYDON

THE study of history is commonly regarded as almost essential to a full education. It figures prominently in school syllabuses; history departments in universities are well populated; publishers' lists are crowded with historical titles; the Taylors and the Bullocks are watched by millions on television. In less tangible ways too, there is ample evidence of the felt importance of history. Politicians and publicists incessantly appeal to the past, ostensibly for guidance or justification. Public opinion constantly assumes that a given course of action is possible or undesirable because it succeeded or failed in the past. Indeed some nations seem to live their lives almost totally in terms of the past: for generations Frenchmen have behaved as if they must try to resolve in their lifetimes issues that first arose in clear form during the great French Revolution. Yet despite all this there are many who doubt the validity of the claims made on behalf of history. According to J. H. Plumb, ninety per cent of historians believe 'that the subject they practise is meaningless in any ultimate sense. . . . Fewer and fewer historians believe that their art has any social purpose: any function as a coordinator of human endeavour or human thought.'[1] If these views are justified, should history continue to play any major role in education?

This curiously uncertain position largely springs from the variety of motives for which history is studied and the extravagance of the claims made for it. These motives and claims fall into roughly three groups.

---

1. 'The Historian's Dilemma', in J. H. Plumb (ed.), *Crisis in the Humanities* (1964), pp. 25-6.

Firstly, men find the study of history fascinating 'for its own sake', in much the same way that fictional works of a certain type fascinate them. This very general phenomenon scarcely needs elaboration, though it is worth noting that it more often leads to an interest in Scott than Stubbs, in a narrative because it is superficially amusing rather than because it is true.

The second group of motives for historical study may be illustrated by an anecdote of Marc Bloch's:

> I had gone with Henri Pirenne to Stockholm; we had scarcely arrived, when he said to me: 'What shall we go to see first? It seems that there is a new city hall here. Let's start there.' Then, as if to ward off my surprise, he added: 'If I were an antiquarian, I would have eyes only for old stuff, but I am a historian. Therefore, I love life.'[2]

The historian's love of life is in fact very often what leads him to the past, and the form which interest in the past takes is conditioned by a variety of present interests which we will discuss below.

It is commonly believed, for example, that the modern world cannot be properly conceived without a knowledge of the past; as Leibniz said, one of the benefits of studying history is discovering 'the origin of things present which are to be found in things past; for a reality is never better understood than through its causes'. Such assumptions lie behind the present spate of books on the origins of the Vietnamese war; and the likely validity of these assumptions is enhanced when we reflect on the massive inertia of social life and on the fact that truly immense changes usually germinate for a long time. Because human evolution does not consist of a series of self-contained jerks, there seems to be considerable point in trying to comprehend the present by examining the past. And even if the past world we choose to examine has very little causal connexion with our own, true understanding of present life is assisted by a comparison of it with quite different systems.

2. Marc Bloch, *The Historian's Craft*, translated by P. Putnam (1954), p. 43.

Alternatively, confident attempts are made to predict future events on the basis of the past, often by analogical reasoning: Hitler consoled himself just before his defeat in 1945 with the thought that Frederick the Great suffered equally great reverses before his triumph in the Seven Years' War. Similarly, some men attempt to draw lessons from the past on which to base their future actions: history is conceived of as philosophy teaching by examples. Voltaire, in 'On the Usefulness of History', enthusiastically advocated this process, even though by the unconscious banality of some of his examples he cast doubt on its value:

> The great errors of the past are also very useful in many ways. One cannot remind oneself too often of crimes and disasters. These, no matter what people say, can be forestalled ... the undoing of Charles XII at Pultawa will warn a general not to plunge deep into the Ukraine without supplies.[3]

But whether we think the process valid or not, it is commonly adopted: presumably some such motive lies behind the many volumes of government-sponsored war histories, and behind the fact that courses for army officers devote considerable attention to the successful tactics of great generals and the errors of bad ones.

A more perverse reason for the study of history is that if one dislikes present reality and sees no chance of changing it, one can always take refuge in a more attractive past. If one is a Frenchman smarting under the defeat of 1870, one can read biographies of Napoleon I. If one is a German of the mid-nineteenth century, disgruntled with the impotent and fragmented condition of Germany, one can read of the War of Liberation from Napoleonic rule in the works of Häusser, Droysen and many others. This explains the popularity of those historical works which raise visions of a distant and more perfect world. Even great histories can contain this element: it pervades histories of the French Revolution, whether the golden age or great man is the

---

3. Parts of the essay are quoted in F. Stern (ed.), *The Varieties of History* (1956), p. 44.

Federation period of 1790 (Michelet), the Constitutional Monarchists (Droz), the Girondins (Lamartine), Danton (Aulard) or Robespierre (Louis Blanc). And the fact that the escapism may be unconscious merely means that such history can be written and read more eagerly, without the guilt that conscious escapism sometimes entails. Similarly, grudges against the present can be worked off by attacking the past, as in Taine's onslaught on the French Revolution and Napoleon.

A related function of history is to justify and glorify one's own life or status by showing the inevitability or rightness of the events which formed one's nation, sect, class, region or race. The classic example is Whig history: Macaulay's *History of England* was probably designed and certainly read as a eulogy for the society to which he belonged and the processes which he thought formed it. Indeed history is often used as a weapon in political struggles. It was said that every volume of Bancroft's *History of the United States* voted for Jackson, and most of the nineteenth-century histories of the French Revolution voted against Charles X, Louis Philippe, Napoleon III or the Third Republic. Much ink was spilt in the inter-war years on the question of whether Imperial Germany was guilty of starting the First World War, as the Treaty of Versailles asserted; and in so far as men believed her to be proved innocent, they felt less inclined to deny the justice of Hitler's attempts to upset the settlements of 1919–23.

But some see in history an even wider reality and value. We cannot talk about our present social and communal life without considering how that life took up its present forms, for those forms are inseparable from the past. It is not just that modern British society is better understood if we know something of the forces extending backwards for thousands of years that made it, but that the past in a certain sense is the present. The communal consciousness has been so deeply moulded by the major events of the past that those events have an existing reality. A hundred plaques and a thousand books remind us of the Smithfield martyrs; the death of Charles I and the overthrowing of James II are not just sources and signs of the anti-dictatorial tendencies in British life, they are existing factors which make it more difficult for the present nature of that life to be changed. History has this role most clearly in France: Napoleon III could not have existed without the immense yearning for Napoleon I, and General de Gaulle occupied a position in the national mind compounded of a tension between the two resolves 'No more Louis XIVs' and 'No more Daladiers'. Of course this almost tangible existence of the past in our lives has drawbacks. Namier said:

> A neurotic, according to Freud, is a man dominated by unconscious memories, fixated on the past, and incapable of overcoming it: the regular condition of human communities. Yet the dead festering past cannot be eliminated by violent action any more than an obsession can be cured by beating the patient. History has therein a 'psycho-analytic' function . . .[4]

But this increases the need for an exact study of history. For if we are, in fact, unconsciously dominated by the past we could attempt to overcome this domination by a clearer understanding of the past and by making explicit what lurks obscurely in our minds, so that the true degree of our subjection can be seen. In this way we would appreciate more precisely what is and is not possible for us, which parts of the past still exist and which do not, which parts of the still existing past can be changed and which cannot.

We have so far considered two groups of reasons for historical study: an interest in the past for its own sake, and an interest in the past springing from the pressures of the present. Our third and final group of reasons for historical study concerns history in a narrower and less widely experienced role than either of the first two – as an intellectual discipline. Just as political publicists incessantly assert that modern society cannot be understood without a knowledge of its past, so educational publicists assert that no other intellectual discipline can properly be understood without

4. L. B. Namier, 'History', *Avenues of History* (1952), p. 5.

a knowledge of the history of earlier developments in it. More importantly, problems of history are interesting to those who specialize in related disciplines: philosophers want to know how and with what legitimacy historians use concepts like 'cause', 'responsible', 'inevitable', 'choice', 'oligarchy', 'capitalist'. And, finally, it is often felt that apart from the information about and understanding of the past a study of history gives, its procedures are something without experience of which one cannot be called fully educated, because those procedures have vigorous and imaginative qualities of great value in dealing with human thought and human life in general.

We have just noted the reasons why men are led to historical study. The main role of a course of history as part of general education should be to scrutinize and evaluate these reasons – to inquire whether the questions men ask of the past can lead to meaningful answers. Some men read historical works as they read those of Baroness Orczy: is that satisfactory? Men draw lessons from the past and predict the future: what is a 'lesson' and has a historical generalization any useful predictive value? Educators advance the claims of history as one of the most essential elements in true education: is it in fact sufficiently rigorous and fruitful compared to other subjects?

How can such a scrutiny be accomplished in a course of history as part of general education? The main dangers in a general treatment of any subject for non-specialists would seem to be superficiality, abstractness and tendentiousness on the part of the teacher, and correspondingly passivity, dependence and uncriticalness on the part of the pupil. Superficiality and abstractness are likely to arise because of the shortage of time; and these are the main vices of one of the most common of general historical courses, the sketch of the main events of human history – 'from Plato to Nato' – which finds its counterpart in book form in H. G. Wells's *Outline of History*. The teacher is likely to be tendentious because he is likely to have a strong point of view about what he teaches, and though a strong point of view is not harmful in itself, the pupil will not necessarily have any means of understanding that what he is told is in fact tendentious. A desire to be passive, dependent and uncritical will often be strong in the pupil, and it is important to attempt to combat this desire and to devise a course which will prevent it arising. The pupil ought to be allowed to realize the tentative, exploratory and sometimes fortuitous nature of historical work.

For these reasons, a course of history as part of general education ought above all to be presented in a critical and provisional way, and should allow the great issues that have perennially agitated historians to be apprehended by pupils personally and directly. These issues raise the fundamental difficulties of history, which are often not apparent to a general reader. He no doubt realizes that great ability and labour is needed to master languages, diplomatic, palaeography, numismatics, archaeology, chronology, genealogy, historical geography and many other ancillary historical tools; but he tends to think that there is no particular difficulty in reading and understanding books about history. Now while all historians have to acquire some of these difficult ancillary skills, the true difficulties of history, which must be grappled with by the general reader, are more fundamental and more general; without such a grappling any historical reading is perhaps worse than worthless. We shall discuss these issues briefly under three heads. Firstly, what dangers are associated with certain *a priori* assumptions historians make? Secondly, what are the problems involved in learning lessons from the past and formulating general laws from past experience? Thirdly, are there limitations or advantages in particular kinds of historical evidence?

With what attitude should historians approach the past? How can we reconcile Ranke's desire to write of past ages 'as they actually were' with Michelet's conception of history as resurrection, or with Dilthey's conception of it as the reliving in the historian's mind of the spiritual activity that originally produced his sources? (The difference between these slogans is a theoretical difference that first became plain in nineteenth-century discussions of how history should be written. Ranke believed the historian should not play the part of prophet or judge, and he coupled with this a concentration on hitherto untouched archival material. His lifetime saw a marked improvement in the critical handling of sources. A view arose that history should be written with complete neutrality – without the intervention of the historian's personality at all; and this contrasted with the idea of history as a resurrection or reliving of the past by the historian.) We may well question whether there is in fact any contradiction between the sound and critical scholarship of a Ranke and the intense life which Michelet breathed into his work. But this debate raises other questions about how the historian should write. Does he merely discover all the available 'facts' on his subject, and then 'interpret' them? Or can the formulation of new problems which triggers off innovations in historical writing arise in a quite fortuitous way? And is not the evolution of what the reader can see is the historian's 'point of view' or 'interpretation' likely to be a slow, almost unconscious process? We can hardly appreciate such problems unless we try to do some historical writing ourselves, on however small a scale.

Apart from this kind of problem, there is also the question of the relationship between the historian's present interests which lead him to the past, and the past as it 'actually' was. Is Ranke's belief that all past ages are of intrinsic importance since all are 'immediate to God' reconcilable with Croce's dictum that 'all history is contemporary history', or with Niebuhr's remark that 'when a historian is reviving former times, his interest in them and sympathy with them will be the deeper, the greater the events he has witnessed [in his own lifetime] with a bleeding or rejoicing heart'?[5] Undoubtedly, since men of the past have at least some emotions and qualities in common with us, we can

5. Barthold Niebuhr, Preface to *History of Rome* (2nd edn), quoted in F. Stern (ed.), *op. cit.*, p. 53.

understand their experiences better by reference to our own.

For here, in the present, is immediately perceptible that vibrance of human life which only a great effort of the imagination can restore to the old texts. I have many times read, and I have often narrated, accounts of wars and battles. Did I truly know, in the full sense of that word, did I know from within, before I myself had suffered the terrible, sickening reality, what it meant for an army to be encircled, what it meant for a people to meet defeat? Before I myself had breathed the joy of victory in the summer and autumn of 1918 (and, although, alas! its perfume will not again be quite the same, I yearn to fill my lungs with it a second time) did I truly know all that was inherent in that beautiful word? In the last analysis, whether consciously or no, it is always by borrowing from our daily experiences and by shading them, where necessary, with new tints that we derive the elements which help us to restore the past.[6]

But can the past be appropriately grasped through our own experiences? We may have no alternative if our histories are to live, but we run the danger of violating the uniqueness of past times. And if the past can only be grasped through present experience, presumably future generations will have to rewrite our histories because their experiences may be different from and richer than ours: can and should there be a 'final history'?

This discussion of the past in terms of present feelings can lead to what has been called the 'Abominable Snowman' fallacy.[7] The Snowman walks backwards with his feet pointing forwards, thus evading his pursuers. Historians who imitate him by examining the past with only the present in mind may blind themselves to things existing in the past but not the present. The fallacy appears in a simple form in the history of law, because a lawyer examining legal history is tempted to be interested only in those parts of ancient

6. Marc Bloch, *op. cit.*, p. 44, written in France between 1940 and the author's execution by the Germans on 16 June 1944 for his Resistance activities.
7. A. W. B. Simpson, 'The Penal Bond with Conditional Defeasance', *Law Quarterly Review*, vol. 82 (1966), p. 392.

law which became modern law, and a dilemma arises: 'The lawyer must be orthodox or he is no lawyer; an orthodox history seems to me a contradiction in terms.'[8] But in more subtle forms the fallacy is a danger for all historians. The danger of 'orthodoxy' arises for the historian every time the past is approached with a rigid and unitary point of view – with *a priori* expectations which dominate the historian. The alternative of trying to immerse oneself in the past without preconceived notions may leave the historian without sound bearings; and since recent periods are generally better known than ancient, it is easier to reason from the known present to the unknown past.

It is worth elaborating on the dangers of orthodoxy, for it covers many traps of which the historian must be wary. It is, for example, a received and almost unchallenged dogma that one of the most indispensable assets for a historian is sympathy with his subject. Since few men can sympathize with what they dislike, historians are often prey to an extension of the Snowman fallacy. That fallacy involved the risk that only what we have experienced in the present will be looked for in the past; its extension involves the more insidious dangers that only what is congenial to us in the present will be discussed in the past, and that what is uncongenial will be misrepresented or ignored. If we believe that sympathy is enough, how do we regard historians like Taine? His works express and are shaped by an intense and passionate hatred for the tendencies of French history from the seventeenth century on, and particularly for the French Revolution; yet is he to be denied a kind of greatness? It seems difficult to overlook the force and value of his work; but his radical challenge to certain complacent assumptions of educated opinion was sneered at in his own day – and in ours, as Pieter Geyl was once embarrassingly reminded.

It happened in 1948, when I attended the last sitting . . . of the great international congress held in Paris and devoted to the

8. F. W. Maitland, 'Why the History of English Law is not written', in H. A. L. Fisher (ed.), *Collected Papers*, vol. I (1911), p. 491.

history of the revolutions of 1848. Professor Labrousse delivered the final lecture. Then, in the discussion, up rose from the back row an old gentleman, bearded all over his face and rather shabbily dressed, who sounded a note that apparently, after a full week of talk, impressed the assembled members as altogether novel. He said that what had struck him in the proceedings was that everybody seemed to have started from the assumption that revolution was 'a good thing'. As for him, he ventured to question this and to urge his hearers to ask themselves whether really revolution was the best method for promoting reform and progress, whether it was not on the contrary an extraordinarily wasteful and risky method, a method always leading to unforeseeable complications and unhappy after-effects. '*Taine*,' he said, and at that name the audience of distinguished French historians, which had turned round to look at the speaker with slightly bored amusement, positively broke into a ripple of laughter. Imagine mentioning Taine, who was a mere interloper, and to mention whom seriously (as Aulard had actually written) would almost cause a candidate for a history degree to be ploughed! I particularly noticed the broad smile and the expressive shrug of the excellent and deservedly famous old Professor Lefebvre.

The speaker was Daniel Halévy, and I confess that my sympathy at that moment was with him. Later on I read his *Histoire d'une histoire* (1939) . . . attacking the cult of the revolutionary tradition as he saw it observed in the official world of French historians (exactly as Lasserre and De Marans had seen it twenty-seven years earlier), and I found the little work very stimulating and instructive. At the same time, how one-sided was the view taken by this same M. Halévy. How blindly he revered, not either Danton or Robespierre, not Mignet or Michelet, but Renan and Taine. And still later on I discovered that M. Halévy had, during the war, been an ardent supporter of Marshal Pétain.[9]

It may be true that a malignant and vicious hatred of the past is ultimately repellent; in Taine's case it entailed something of a waste of his great gifts as a historian. Certainly the Balzac–Taine–Halévy tradition had disastrous political

9. Pieter Geyl, 'French Historians for and against the Revolution', in *Encounters in History* (1961), pp. 140–41.

consequences, substantial immediate causes of which were the shabby moral and intellectual compromises characteristic of the Halévys when they backed Pétain, or preferred Hitler to Léon Blum. But if one aim of education is to challenge received and uncriticized assumptions, and if historians are to hold themselves open to the fullness of past reality, a course of history for general education should inquire whether sympathy is enough. In some circumstances, hatred may be better than a blindly confident acceptance of some features of the past. At least the presence of such emotions means that elements in the past will be examined which would be excluded if a purely sympathetic approach is adopted.

On the other hand, another example of the dangers of orthodoxy is approaching the past with a certain moral point of view. Should moral judgements be made on the past? If one judges the past in terms of some agreed present-day morality, one tends to distort the reality of the past. Our morality may have been impossibly strict for men of the past, or unknown to them; other choices than the ones we think good may have been necessary. Can one condemn the Spanish Inquisition too harshly when almost all sects in that age dealt with heresy cruelly and violently? But if the historian judges the past on its own terms, he may find himself being taken to approve things he hates, and a fear of this coupled with a felt obligation to sympathize with the past may lead to a rather grey objectivity. And which of the diverse sets of moral standards prevailing in a past age should be chosen as the standard of judgement for that age? But the alternative of complete neutrality in discussing the past may be very difficult to achieve, if only because we apprehend and discuss so much of life in moral terms.

Similarly there is the problem of bias. The historian is almost always at least unconsciously biased – affected by prejudices and interests which may be inappropriate in discussing the past. Possibly the adverse effects of such bias can be avoided, either by frank acknowledgement of them by the historian himself, or by the reader taking them into account. But is bias in fact pernicious? It can be argued that a history written without bias or passion would be lifeless and therefore useless. This raises the further question whether history is best written by men who have lived through the events they describe, or by men of later generations who can place events in perspective. There are certainly famous examples of works which are partly memoirs, partly contemporary history, like the histories of Machiavelli, Guicciardini or Clarendon, or the *Memoirs* of de Tocqueville – statesmen who actually took part in some of the events which they describe. On the other hand, has contemporaneity any advantage apart from that? The greatest, even the most vivid, histories seem to be written by later generations.

Another orthodoxy among historians is the assumption that only those men, creeds and forces that triumphed, that made the modern world, are worth discussing, so that the 'losers' are mentioned only briefly. Thus the Jacobins are discussed more than Mirabeau, totalitarian thinkers like Marx more than the anarchists, and the Bolsheviks more than the Mensheviks. We may ask: should the role of the losers be discussed more? How legitimately can we consider what choices were open to past men? Are the conscious motives of past men important? Can they be psychoanalysed? How important is the dispute between free will and determinism? Can individuals alone influence the course of history?

These questions raise one great problem for the historian. The natural scientist can apprehend reality by repeated controlled experiments, but historical evidence cannot be so tested. We cannot examine the French Revolution through a microscope and say: our first experiment showed what happened after Mirabeau's death, our second will assume that Mirabeau lived another ten years, our third will assume that Robespierre was never born. Historians do in fact consider what might have occurred but did not, but they do so with less confidence than a natural scientist. The sociologist attempts to overcome this problem of the impossibility of controlled experiments on human affairs by critical thought about the collection and analysis of his data – the selection of samples on statistically sound principles, for example. The historian attempts by any available means to estimate the power of opposing forces in a given situation: he tries to say whether the dislike of Mirabeau by royal circles, and the future power of the Girondins and Jacobins outweighed Mirabeau's own abilities and established strength, so that the Revolution could have continued as it in fact did even if Mirabeau had lived. Only in this way can the possible role of the unforeseen contingency be hinted at. And it is important to do this, for unless some sense is given of the uncertainty and doubt that past men actually experienced, a false feeling of inevitability may arise and the life of the age may seem impoverished and dull. We know the outcome of the 1848 revolutions, but the men of 1848 did not, and the atmosphere of 1848 is evoked falsely if failure seems inevitable from the outset.

A final example of the dangers of historical orthodoxy is suggested by Tolstoy's pessimistic remark: 'History will never reveal to us what connexions there are, and at what times, between science, art and morality, between good and evil, religion and the civic virtues. . . .' Certainly historians have found these tasks difficult, as Tolstoy's savage parody of school histories of the French Revolution indicates:

Louis XIV was a very proud and self-confident man. He had such and such mistresses, and such and such ministers, and they governed France badly. The heirs of Louis XIV were also weak men, and also governed France badly. They also had such and such favourites and such and such mistresses. Besides which, certain persons were at this time writing books. By the end of the eighteenth century there must have gathered in Paris two dozen or so persons who started saying that all men were free and equal. Because of this in the whole of France people began to slaughter and drown each other.[10]

Everyone now follows J. R. Green's denunciation of drum and trumpet history, and it is agreed that political history

10. *War and Peace*, Epilogue, Part II, Chapter 1.

alone is not the key to the past, but other unitary keys have been offered. It is important that the value and role of such divisions as national history, economic history and ecclesiastical history should be scrutinized; an age may be totally distorted if only one aspect of its life is examined, for other aspects may contradict it but be related to it in a seemingly strange way. Just as Hitler loved Eva Braun and was kind to animals, so societies apparently based on respect for humanity may countenance gross evils, and one form of behaviour may be a sort of compensation for the other. A related error can arise with periodization. Ideally the selected period will have some organic connexion with the historian's subject-matter, which will suggest its own proper period. Diplomatic histories of Europe from Bach to Bartok are not written, but there are scarcely less absurd examples of national histories written between the often irrelevant dates of the coronations of monarchs or the installation of governments.

The second group of great historical issues which we will mention involves the question of lessons from the past, prediction and generalization. Can lessons be learnt from history? In political debate, it is often said they can. Eden justified his Suez policy by the need to avoid the error of appeasing dictators, said to have been made by British and French statesmen in the 1930s, and the same justification is often advanced for American foreign policy since 1945. Of course, such arguments usually attempt to rationalize decisions taken for other reasons; and the differences between the situations politicians have to deal with will often preclude the confident learning of lessons, which may in any case be too vague to be useful. Great errors have been made by applying the supposed lessons of history. The war of movement thought to have been developed by Napoleon I became *de rigueur* for the French Staff after 1870 and led to disastrous losses in 1914; accordingly French leaders evolved the Maginot doctrine of defensive war and applied it in 1940, but by then a war of movement had again become possible, and over short periods irresistible, as the

German victories of that year showed. Whether lessons can be learnt from the past is a question that can only be decided by comparing actual situations and not on *a priori* grounds alone.

Can general historical laws with predictive value be formulated? The critic may be able to destroy quite easily the general historical laws and the predictions based on them of such prophets of doom or joy as Condorcet, Marx, H. S. Chamberlain, Gobineau, Spengler, Toynbee and Sorokin. But the efforts of these system-makers raise the question whether more limited laws may not be justifiable. No ready agreement is to be found on this issue, or on a related dispute between sociologists and historians. Historians are often urged to consider 'the aspects of the event that reveal the major dynamics of the culture, the uniformities rather than those features that appear to be most colourful or unique'.[11] The representative retort is:

> The particular quality of history that gives it its real worth, that places it more than any other discipline at the centre of life, shall always lie in just this fact: that history conceives of and treats its material as events, not as organisms. The sociologist and the psychologist are concerned mainly that the facts of a case conform to a system of ideas; for the historian this conformity has little or no importance – indeed, the term 'case' does not belong in history at all.[12]

Even if prediction is impossible or doubtful, historical discourse would be difficult without the invention of generalizing words to describe similar events and institutions – '*coups d'état*', 'revolutions' and so on. This is a process to be adopted only with care. Arnold once said of Macaulay that there are some styles in which it is impossible to tell the truth. 'Style' of course goes beyond purely formal or external considerations, and in this sense there lurk grave dangers for the historian as he thinks and writes. He may begin by using technical terms like 'capitalism' quite neutrally, but

11. T. Cochran, 'The Social Sciences and the Problem of Historical Synthesis', in F. Stern (ed.), *op. cit.*, p. 353.
12. J. Huizinga, 'The Idea of History', *ibid.*, p. 291.

such terms can gradually take on an emotive life of their own until they become uncontrolled monsters running amok in the historian's work. A similar process occurs with even larger metaphors: everything that conflicted with Oswald Spengler's scheme for the interpretation of human history in *The Decline of the West* was discarded without explanation. Historians cannot do without certain key words like Renaissance, Middle Ages, reaction, revolution; but all such words have acquired approving or disapproving overtones of which the historian must attempt to be conscious: if the historian's language or theories cease to be regarded by him merely as provisional tools, to be discarded if necessary, and come to dominate his work, they distort the past. A further danger is that the same words are often used by men of different periods with different meanings: 'there were bishops in the fourth century, and party names were in use in eighteenth-century England; yet conclusions must not be drawn from either fact without a thorough understanding of what those terms then covered'.[13]

The third main set of problems for the historian have to do with his evidence. What are the main limitations on the historian's evidence? He has to contend with deliberate misrepresentation in the memoirs of statesmen, or in state documents written and published with one eye on posterity, for example the various coloured books of foreign policy documents published by the powers after the outbreak of the Second World War. He must remember that certain types of evidence involve fictions, particularly legal records and medieval financial records. Some evidence is indeed more valuable than might at first appear, for example imaginative literature.

A real literary interest is an interest in man, society and civilization, and its boundaries cannot be drawn. . . . If, for instance, we want to go further than the mere constatation that a century and a half ago the family counted for much more than it does now, if we want some notion of the difference involved in day-to-

13. L. B. Namier, *op. cit.*, p. 3.

day living – in the sense of life and its dimensions and in its emotional and moral accenting – for the ordinary cultivated person, we may profitably start trying to form it from the novels of Jane Austin. But only if we are capable of appreciating shade, tone, implication and essential structure.[14]

Indeed literature, in which a culture can have its most intense expression, seems an indispensable source if rightly used. In extreme contrast, a source like palaeographical evidence about the writing and transmission of manuscripts can tell us, as no other source could, of the education and organization of a society. There are of course features of the past which conventional sources will never tell us because they did not interest or seem remarkable to the compilers of the sources. But they can be reconstructed by a process of imaginative inference of this kind:

To the world when it was half a thousand years younger, the outlines of all things seemed more clearly marked than to us. The contrast between suffering and joy, between adversity and happiness, appeared more striking. All experiences had yet to the minds of men the directness and absoluteness of the pleasure and pain of child-life. . . . Calamities and indigence were more afflicting than at present; it was more difficult to guard against them, and to find solace. Illness and health presented a more striking contrast; the cold and darkness of winter were more real evils. Honours and riches were relished with greater avidity and contrasted more vividly with surrounding misery. We, at the present day, can hardly understand the keenness with which a fur coat, a good fire on the hearth, a soft bed, a glass of wine, were formerly enjoyed.[15]

How can the pupil be brought face to face with these issues so that he feels them as the great historians have felt them? Though no doubt human life is always changing, there are certain periods when the rate of change accelerates, when, at least for certain groups, life is lived with a new and peculiar intensity, when old forms of society and

14. F. R. Leavis, 'Sociology and Literature', *The Common Pursuit* (1952), pp. 200–203.
15. J. Huizinga, *The Waning of the Middle Ages* (1924), p. 9.

structures of belief are shattered or radically challenged, when some rebellious gesture seemingly no different from countless earlier unsuccessful gestures suddenly begins an era of violent change and life appears to hold out attractive choices never noticed or possible before. In Western European history, three such periods were the Reformation era, the age of the American and French Revolutions, and the period between 1914 and 1941. From any point of view such a period is appropriate for study as part of general education. These periods have great intrinsic interest, they raise fundamental questions about how historians ought to discuss and categorize them, discussion of them is bound to suggest comparison with our age, and each of them was probably of vital importance in moulding modern society – of much greater importance than more trivial if more recent events. Take the Reformation. The events of the sixteenth century have an immense fascination: an irrevocable shattering of the political and religious unity of Europe, a sudden outburst of violent social revolution, striking new developments in political, social and religious thought, a gradual growth of despotic central power in some states, a decline of Europe into a state of almost continual war. The most intense controversies divide historians as to the deeper causes and long-term effects of the Reformation; and at the heart of these controversies lie the crucial historiographical issues outlined above.

In the case of the Reformation, a course of history for general education could be based on a series of lectures that would raise the problems thought most important, coupled with a series of seminars in which these problems, and problems encountered by pupils in their own reading, could be discussed more fully and personally. That reading would begin with general works like Volume II of the *New Cambridge Modern History*, collections of documents like Elton's *Renaissance and Reformation* and more specialized collections like Kitch's *Capitalism and the Reformation* and Kidd's *Documents Illustrative of the Continental Reformation* (which might be supplemented by further cyclostyled collections of documents). At first, the following sorts of question might be discussed: was Luther merely a more extreme Erasmus, interested only in extirpating abuses, or did he regard the Church as being fundamentally in error? Was Erasmus a Kerensky to Luther's Lenin – did Erasmus lay the egg and Luther hatch it, as the common sixteenth-century saying had it? How far did the sixteenth-century Protestant movements, which were often irrational and mystical, with deep pietistic roots, lead to such modern-seeming ideals as freedom of thought and religion, or to such developments as the scientific revolution? Was the increasing power of monarchs genuinely new, or was it merely that in the sixteenth century kings seemed so strong because in the fifteenth they had been so weak? How far were the popular radical social movements due to Luther? How far was the Reformation a predominantly spiritual movement? Were political factors in reality paramount – German princes against the Emperor or the Turk, Dutch nationalism against Spanish imperialism, the French king against the Emperor, secular states attempting to overthrow the temporal power of the Papacy? Was the Reformation after it began a fully spontaneous movement or a state-controlled one? (In England Henry VIII tried to control the Reformation politically, but failed to keep step with popular opinion, as the reaction to conservative measures like the Act of the Six Articles shows. On the other hand Mary's accession was popular with substantial elements of the people. There are in fact few sixteenth-century examples of a ruler different in religion from the majority of his people, either because rulers generally thought their kingdoms worth a mass or because parts of the peoples were willing to alter their external practices to suit the state.) Did economic and social factors have primacy – price inflation, or the revolt of peasants against the abolition of ancient rights (for example, by enclosure)? Was the Reformation the manifestation of the economic interests of a rising bourgeoisie? What was the true connexion between the Reformation and capitalism?

Pupils would be referred to the crucial works that discuss these issues, but they would simultaneously be considering deeper questions about bias, periodization and the problems of definition – e.g. what was sixteenth-century capitalism? A prominent question would be the role of the individual and his unconscious motivation: are the attempts of Grisar and Denifle to prove Luther mad or perverted relevant in considering the truth of his beliefs or his historical importance? What is the value of Erikson's psycho-analysis of Luther in *Young Man Luther*? We know a great deal about Luther, but Erikson really only finds useful a few remarks made by Luther in his old age about events occurring decades earlier; can characters of whom we know far less be similarly psycho-analysed? The issues of how far the past moulds the present, and of lessons and predictions drawn from the past would arise in considering whether Luther can in any sense be said to be responsible for Hitler, and whether Charles V's dealings with Lutheranism, or the attempted defence of Western Europe against the Turk are of any importance for the making of foreign policy in our day. The famous debate initiated by Max Weber and Werner Sombart about the relationship between capitalism and the Reformation could lead to a discussion about whether the methods of sociology are a valuable addition to those of history. Each pupil might be asked to write a long essay on a problem of this kind. It would not involve original work in the sense of reference to unprinted sources or sources which no historian had ever handled before. Nor would it be original from a professional historian's point of view, or in the sense that it deserved publication (though this would not be excluded). But it would not mean a summarized reproduction of the contents of a reading list. The pupil would be given suggestions by the teacher as to where he should start his reading, but he would follow up and verify his ideas alone. In short, the essay, if it were to be written competently, would require genuinely independent and original thought as far as the pupil is concerned.

As the pupil reflects on the period, he may become conscious of the extreme difficulty of historical analysis and the great tact needed in characterizing past ages. Many of those religious practices usually thought characteristic of the Counter-Reformation existed before the Reformation. Savonarola's reaction against Renaissance worldliness is found earlier in the fifteenth century: the burning of articles of luxury under the guidance of famous preachers was common. Lutheranism no doubt flourished because of sixteenth-century anti-clericalism, but anti-clericalism pervaded the later Middle Ages even when this co-existed with frequent outbursts of ardent piety. The social impulses of the sixteenth century do not seem so uniquely a Renaissance or Protestant achievement when we remember that one element in the medieval ideal of chivalry was pity for the poor.

One problem that study of the Reformation era raises is that much of human activity was motivated by considerations that have little reality for us. To few of us, Christian or not, are the issues in the transubstantiation controversy alive; and while articulate fifteenth-century men thought the most important aspect of their age was chivalry, we find it one of the least real. Are we then to overlook all those elements alien to us?

This would be so if, to understand the spirit of an age, it sufficed to know its real and hidden forces and not its illusions, its fancies and its errors. But for the history of civilization every delusion or opinion of an epoch has the value of an important fact.[16]

In considering the Reformation, we may come to understand the value and the necessity of sympathy with the past.

One teaching device that may help towards an appreciation of the ambiguity and confused richness of the past is as follows. A pupil might be invited to defend a briefly stated and possibly extreme though arguable thesis about the Reformation and debate publicly with a critic of it. Such a thesis might be: 'The sixteenth century witnessed a disastrous shattering of the tenuous medieval balance in both Church and State. It led to a decline in tolerance, ushered

16. *ibid.*, p. 57.

in a century of bloody religious wars, and in encouraging the new forces of centralized state power and nationalism led to those evils that reached their peak in the wars of the late nineteenth and twentieth century. The scientific, inquiring spirit of the age, the growth of an individualist ethos, and the advancing capitalism of the period led only to a mindless pursuit of material objects that ultimately brutalized mankind and brought us to our present position on the edge of the abyss.'

No one of course should be asked at the outset to defend a thesis he does not believe in or sympathize with. But such a debate would be most instructive in showing how difficult it is to agree on what 'actually happened', and in showing how the different views that can exist about the past arise and can be defended; it would suggest how differences could be overcome by reference to new evidence and the clarification of rival modes of reasoning and moral judgement. In the later stages of the debate the contestants would be challenged by the teacher and other members of the class, and the teacher may well make it his business both here and in more orthodox seminars to introduce confusion, if he thinks it appropriate, into unduly complacent and neatly organized minds. At all events, debates of this kind ('moots') have been an important and successful part of English legal education for centuries. By methods of this kind we can hope to overcome the passivity and uncriticalness which we saw to be a possible danger in general education.

The teacher would have little difficulty in devising a similar course for the French Revolution, the 1914–41 period, or any other period or subject he thought fit. The main need is to stress an independent and individual approach by pupils in their seminars, essays, debates and in their own reading. The course could be modified depending on the age and sophistication of the pupils and the available library resources. Indeed, a courageous and interested person could derive some of the benefits of such a course out of his own independent reading with only occasional suggestions from a teacher.

It is to be hoped that some such course is practicable in terms of time and of teaching and financial resources. History has an often deserved reputation as a soft option, and a coffee-table blight faces the general reader seeking to understand the past. But in fact the subject raises the most difficult and important questions about human nature and human society. Historical reasoning has general interest when compared with formal and informal logic, scientific method, the judgement of literature, and the methods of subjects closely related to history like archaeology, sociology and anthropology: an appreciation of the nature of historical reasoning, which at an introductory level could be obtained from the course outlined, would be of great general value.

But the main value of the course is this. Like a harlot, history is at everybody's disposal. Appeals to the past as a means of solving present problems are regularly made in modern organized society. Can history provide the answers men seek? Men often ask the wrong questions of history and are disappointed by their failure to get satisfactory answers. The properly organized study of history as part of general education would teach men not to expect past events to repeat themselves infallibly, nor to predict the future on the basis of very fragmentary evidence, nor to draw 'lessons' from the past because of chance similarities. It would perhaps prevent them from evading the realities of the present by immersion into an idealized and extinct past. It would teach men to escape from or to preserve the past by helping them understand exactly how heavy the forces of the past are in relation to forces for change, without leading them to underestimate the difficulties of genuinely radical change.

Sociology

JENNIFER PLATT

SOCIOLOGY is already frequently taught to non-specialists of various kinds, and it clearly has much to offer them even when not taught as a rigorous discipline. The very fact of the existence of sociology offers a special kind of intellectual challenge: the idea that society can be studied in a relatively objective way and that description can be separated from prescription, and that in the course of this study one may find that things are not as they seem, or that one's own experiences and perceptions of society are not typical, is disturbing to ideological preconceptions and inconsistent with the normal working assumptions of everyday life. Thus an introduction to even the more elementary kinds of social research can help create a critical approach to sloppy generalizations and unexamined assumptions, and to compare one's own experience with research results can start an understanding of the nature and scope of scientific method. In my own life, for instance, it was an intellectual turning point to learn that in financial terms the middle classes had benefited more than the working classes from the National Health Service, since this simple fact from research made it impossible to continue to hold a set of attitudes about the welfare state which were based on ill-informed current prejudices. Similarly, to learn that members of different social classes typically perceive the class structure differently immediately makes it clear that there may not be such a thing as a 'correct' picture of it, and that even if there is common sense is unlikely to be able to provide it; to learn that the average I.Q.s of American Negro school children improve for each year that they have spent in the North destroys common stereotypes about both race and the nature of innate ability; to learn that the suicide rates of countries, and of social groups within them, differ from each other while themselves remaining rather stable from one year to another makes it clear that even apparently very individualistic forms of action may require social rather than psychological explanations. Thus social subject-matter has the capacity to help arouse a spirit of critical inquiry and examination of assumptions, in addition to its obvious relevance to the general education of any citizen.

So-called (or even not 'so-called') sociology is in practice more commonly taught to non-specialists for a different reason: it is thought to be vocationally or academically useful to them to learn a range of social facts, generally about situations in which they will be working. These social facts are usually taught with a view to equipping the student with the skills of manipulation and social engineering. Thus managers are taught about the attitudes of industrial workers and the ways in which they are related to productivity, and social workers are taught about class differences in family structure and norms. Whether or not one views particular kinds of social manipulation with approval, and whether or not the kind of teaching usually given actually has the intended effect on the students, it is obvious that the knowledge of such social facts is likely to be more useful to those involved than ignorance of them. Some of the factors which may make it less useful than could be expected are discussed later. Another vocational motive for teaching 'sociology', probably of a rather different sort, is the desire to communicate some elements of a research technique that may subsequently be applied in a job situation; this may well be feasible and valuable, but of course techniques of data-collection in isolation do not constitute sociology even if taught by sociologists. Finally, sociology is quite often taught as a subsidiary subject to students whose main work is in another subject, and here there are two broad alternatives: it is taught because it is felt to be closely related to the main subject, generally another social science; or it is taught because it is felt to throw light on the main subject without being closely related to it, as when the sociology of art is taught to art students. In these circumstances sociology unquestionably has something to offer, but how far this is really available to the students will depend on the precise nature of the course; if it is a general or multi-purpose course its relevance may not be apparent or appreciated, particularly for the latter kind of student.

So far, therefore, it can be concluded that sociologists can perform a valuable educational function for non-specialists, although this will not necessarily entail teaching them real sociology, let alone teaching them to be themselves in any sense sociologists, and the same function could sometimes equally well be performed by members of another discipline. But just because sociology is in some ways so obviously relevant there is a temptation for the teacher to take the easy path of offering a soft and unprofessional account of his subject, and for the student to misinterpret what he is told in the light of his pre-existing interests and personal experience.

To state the issue in this way implies a conception of what is and is not properly regarded as being sociology. Abstract definitions are seldom useful for conveying a meaning of this kind, so a more discursive statement will be attempted; this is a necessary preliminary to discussion of how it should be taught. Here as elsewhere it is useful to distinguish between an area of subject-matter and the characteristics of a discipline, although in most of the usual academic 'subjects' the two are intricately associated. In the case of sociology, its subject-matter is in principle the whole of social life, whatever that may mean. In practice, some areas have been much more studied than others by people calling themselves sociologists, so that a description of their activities might lead one to some such statement as this: 'On the whole, the subject-matter of sociology consists mainly of family relationships, class structure, suicide, small groups and productivity in industry, juvenile delinquent gangs, small community characteristics, and voting behaviour, all of them in advanced industrial countries in the twentieth century.' This is plainly an unhelpful statement; in particular, it gives no clue whether *any* study of such subject-matter is inherently sociological or not, or whether study of other subjects can be meaningfully described as sociological. Its only function is to provide demarcation lines between sociology and social anthropology, history, economics and so on; it doesn't even do this in a satisfactory way. Yet implied definitions that take this sort of form are not uncommon among non-sociologists; I have seen Richard Hoggart referred to as a sociologist in an American publisher's blurb, and a professor of economics suggests, as a working rule, that 'aspects of social organization that involve transactions in money are within the province of economics, those that do not are within the province of sociology'.[1] This quotation points to the crucial difficulty in the use of such definitions; most sociologists would regard monetary transactions as well within their sphere – for instance, one of the classic starting points in sociology has been a consideration of the non-contractual elements implied in contracts. But the sociologist is not interested in the same *aspects* of the monetary transaction as the economist is; in practice, each of them abstracts from the complex total reality, and considers only some parts of it.

A further objection may be made to the kind of descriptive account of the subject-matter of sociology offered above, and this is that it makes no explicit reference to any of the more general theorizing done by sociologists; sociologists do study family relationships, but they attempt, for example, to elucidate causal connexions between them and the structure of the economy; they study class structure not merely empirically, but in order to establish general propositions about the functional necessity of social stratification; they study small groups in industry, but they use this study together with that of other groups in order to arrive at generalizations that aspire to apply to all small groups of

1. D. C. Marsh (ed.), *The Social Sciences: An Outline for the Intending Student* (1965).

any kind. This sort of intellectual activity can only with great difficulty be described at all in terms of concrete areas of subject-matter, since its aim is precisely to transcend the concrete particulars in order to arrive at true generalizations covering many sets of particulars. Thus, even if one is only describing what people calling themselves sociologists do, this approach is inadequate, although it may be a necessary starting-point.

Can we, then, distinguish those *aspects* of concrete subject-matter with which sociologists typically concern themselves? There seems to be fairly general agreement among introductory textbooks[2] that sociology has two main distinguishing characteristics. The first is that it is concerned with *social* action and relationships, and not with their biological or psychological aspects. The emphasis on the social means that sociologists look for social *explanations* of social phenomena; thus if, for instance, a sociologist is studying suicide, he will not be interested in the possible role of mental illness in causing suicides, unless that mental illness is itself to some extent socially caused; if mental illness has an effect, but is distributed in a way that seems to be socially random, he will leave that aspect of the study of suicide to a psychologist. The second distinguishing characteristic of sociology is that it is concerned particularly with the inter-relationships among the parts of social wholes. The meaning of this can be clarified by considering what different social science disciplines might tell us about a community. The historian would probably talk about major public events and general social trends in the past; the psychologist would talk about characteristics such as authoritarianism or prejudice, about child-rearing practices and their consequences for patterns of personality development, and about mental illness; the economist would talk about the local industries and occupational structure, and the relationship of the local economy to that of other communities

2. e.g. K. Davis, *Human Society* (1966), p. 9; H. M. Johnson, *Sociology: a Systematic Introduction* (1961), p. 2; A. Inkeles, *What is Sociology?* (1964), p. 16.

and of the country as a whole; the political scientist would talk about power structure and patterns of voting behaviour. The sociologist would be to some extent interested in aspects of all these things, but would be particularly likely to try to work out the causal relationships between the social parts treated separately by other disciplines; he would suggest, for instance, that certain kinds of experience at work lead parents to adopt specific styles of child-rearing, or that political parties are now performing functions for their members that used to be performed by religious organizations, or that changes in the local power structure are attributable to changes in the occupational structure brought about by technological developments. Of course it is not impossible that members of other disciplines will make these same points, but they are not to the same extent committed in principle to doing so.

Sociology as a discipline has come to imply not only the theoretical interests sketched in above, but also a particular set of methods and style of investigation. (The social survey is a technique often seen as strongly associated with sociology, but I think that the association is a superficial one; although the survey is often used by sociologists, its disadvantages are widely recognized and it has no inherent connexion with their intellectual concerns.) The two significant elements of method that I have in mind are the comparative approach to data collection, and a style of data interpretation based on 'multivariate analysis' as a substitute for experiment.

The necessity for the comparative approach arises from the nature of the sociologist's task: given the diversity of societies and of individual human beings, generalizations about them can only confidently be regarded as established when they are based on the examination of a diversity of cases. If the same general statement holds true of bureaucracies in contemporary Britain and ancient China, it is more likely than if only one of them had been studied that it will also hold true of bureaucracies in other societies. Given, however, that societies are diverse, it may not be possible on some issues to make single generalizations that are true of all of them; it then becomes necessary to classify them into types such that true generalizations can be made about all the societies classified as belonging to any one type. At present, for instance, there is some controversy about whether 'industrial society' constitutes a valid type in this sense.[3] It can only be found out how wide the scope of a potential generalization is, and what typology of units is the most useful, by doing the appropriate research; thus there is a continual movement back and forth between the general and the particular, the comparative and the case study, and this dialectical process is very noticeable in the development of sociological thought.

'Multivariate analysis' is a style of analysis that has been worked out in detail in connexion with the analysis of survey results, but it is applicable to any quantitative data where more than one item of information is available about each unit studied. (When the number of units studied becomes small, it shades over imperceptibly into qualitative comparative analysis.) It consists simply in holding constant successive variables in order to assess the effect of one of them (the 'independent' variable) on another (the 'dependent' variable). We can illustrate the nature of this process, at a very simple level, by an imaginary but plausible example. Let us suppose that voting behaviour is being studied, and that in a given election fifty per cent of the voters have voted Left. We wish to know *why* they have voted Left, and so we examine their characteristics further. We know that the Left party has historically associated itself with the interests of the working class, and so we look at the effects of class; dividing the voters crudely into those with manual and those with white-collar occupations, we find indeed that seventy per cent of the manual workers, and only twenty per cent of the white-collar, voted Left. But we know that a higher proportion of men than of women are manual workers, and so we suspect that sex may be confusing the

3. See P. Halmos (ed.), *The Sociological Review Monograph No. 8: The Development of Industrial Societies* (1964).

issue. It is necessary, therefore, to hold sex constant too, and the table below shows what we find. Women do vote Left considerably less often than men in the same sort of occupation, although within each sex there are still large

Proportion voting Left (per cent)

	men	women	total
manual	80	50	70
white-collar	30	10	20
total	65	30	

occupational differences. But why should women vote less Left than men? One hypothesis is that women are more conservative because their child-rearing task has forced them so often to take on the role of the upholder of the established order. If this is true, women who have brought up children should be more conservative than those who have not; and so, for that matter, should men, since they generally play some role in child-rearing too, though a lesser one. We need, therefore, to see if there are any differences between those who have and have not had children, and the next table shows what we find. So far, our expectations are con-

Proportion voting Left (per cent)

	men		women		total
	with children	no children	with children	no children	
manual	75	90	40	65	70
white-collar	25	40	5	20	20
total	60	75	25	40	

firmed; in every case those with children vote Left somewhat less often, and the difference is greater among women. But can this difference really be attributed to the experience of bringing up children? The older someone is, the more likely he is to have had children, and it is known that the average expectancy of life is higher for women than it is for men, so this might really be an age effect . . . and so on.[4] This technique provides the researcher with a means of assessing the importance of the variables he is interested in, even when he does not have the means of isolating them in an experimental situation.

Thus my argument is that the central parts of the sociological tradition are a certain kind of theoretical preoccupation, and a certain methodological style appropriate to such theoretical preoccupations. No one has learnt any sociology who does not have some minimum acquaintance with this complex intellectual tradition, in addition to an acquaintance with some of the main findings of sociological research.

Sociology, as I have suggested earlier, by its nature creates certain special problems for the teacher. Because it is often concerned with matters of which most people have some experience in their everyday lives, everyone is likely to regard himself as already an expert on it. For students without a very strong stake in particular beliefs, this faith can relatively easily be shaken by acquaintance with some research results. I have tried out on a group of first-year university students a list of twelve questions about matters of fact reasonably established by sociological research, and found that the average number of correct answers was five, with a maximum score of seven. (Admittedly, most of the questions were chosen for the paradoxical or commonsensically surprising nature of their answers!) Once this sort of point has been made, research results tend to be taken so seriously that the importance of a critical approach to them needs to be emphasized.

Where students have a strong stake in a particular set of

4. Simple discussions of multivariate analysis in general are hard to find. The locus classicus is P. F. Lazarsfeld, 'Interpretation of Statistical Relations as a Research Operation', in P. F. Lazarsfeld and M. Rosenberg (eds), *The Language of Social Research* (1955); a more recent discussion is available in J. Galtung, *Theory and Methods of Social Research* (1967).

beliefs, however, simple introduction to evidence in favour of alternatives may not be sufficient, at any rate in the short run, or may be sufficient in the short run only to lose its force once they leave the academic context and return to the situation where the original beliefs were established and are often socially supported. An additional difficulty is that a teacher who puts too strong an emphasis on evidence contrary to the student's beliefs, for however respectable a pedagogical motive, is likely to be discredited as himself biased. (Moreover, it is possible that the accusation may be in a sense correct, even if the teacher's points are grounded on the available evidence; there is some reason to believe that to study society is in itself a non-conservative activity that tends to recruit people with non-conservative values, who then undertake research on topics that seem to them interesting and important, which without intentional distortion tends to support their views.) Any teacher of industrial sociology will have some stories to tell about the difficulty of conveying to mature managers that, from the point of view of sociology, the workers' perception of a situation is just as likely to be correct as the managers', and that to treat 'restrictive practices' as a problem to be *solved* is to go beyond the scope of sociology as a social science. Students of all kinds can find it very hard to grasp that a social or personal 'problem' is not necessarily an intellectual problem to the sociologist, and may indeed be banal or irrelevant to him in his capacity as sociologist, even if important to him as a citizen. I have spent several hours trying to explain why, although I agreed that lack of internationalism was deplorable, I did not think that its existence created an intellectual problem, and indeed thought that it was the much more unusual phenomenon of being internationally-minded that required explanation. It is hard to be obliged to tell a warm-hearted student, who cares intensely about the problems of neglected old people and spends his spare time on social work to help them, that his feeling of the importance of the problem does not correspond to its numerical importance, since available statistics show that most old people who need it are looked after by their children. It is not a simple task to defend oneself against the onslaught of a beginning Marxist who regards every reference to social consensus rather than conflict as an example of bourgeois ideology – especially when in many cases one thinks that he is right.

These examples make a number of different points. Firstly, the teacher wants to convey, both in general principle and in particular cases, that the appropriate way in which to resolve a doubt or disagreement about a question of fact is to refer to evidence drawn from systematic research. Then, although the research must be evaluated in a critical spirit, it has to be recognized that relevant data may appear even in work that one disapproves of on academic or value grounds, and that even the ideologically soundest writers sometimes do careless research or make unwarrantably sweeping generalizations from their data; the task of detailed technical assessment cannot be avoided. Next, the distinction between the intellectual and the practical problem must be maintained. There is no reason at all why anyone should not choose to interest himself solely in practical problems, but if he does so he is likely to contribute to sociology only by accident, and will not necessarily find the answers to the questions he wants to ask in the work of sociologists. This does not mean that sociology as such has nothing to contribute to the solution of practical problems, but that its contribution does not always come from a direct study of them, nor does it need to be motivated originally by that kind of interest in order to make this contribution. For an example of this, Peter Townsend, in the course of a fiery critique of British sociology for its lack of concern with problems of social welfare, mentions as an instance of what he condemns one sociologist's paper on 'Protestantism and Capitalism in Sixteenth-Century Germany'.[5] I do not know what became of this particular piece of research, but the whole discussion about Max Weber's thesis on the

5. N. Mackenzie (ed.), *Conviction* (1958): P. Townsend, 'A society for people', p. 104.

causal relationship between the development of Protestantism and of capitalism[6] is now highly relevant to economists' efforts to find ways to improve the situation of underdeveloped countries. A contribution to sociological theory may have implications for many different social problems; a study of one such problem only has broader implications if it is treated theoretically. This point has to be emphasized because of the common confusion between sociology and social work, which springs no doubt partly from the similarity in the sound of the words, but also partly from the characteristic misunderstanding by non-members of the academic community about the ethos of the pursuit of knowledge as an end in itself. Finally, even where sociology does have a direct contribution to make towards the solution of a practical problem, it is likely to be very much a contribution towards it rather than a full answer to the problem as stated.

Vocational students, whose motivation is strictly practical, are particularly likely to look at what is taught to them with a view to finding easy formulae which can be automatically applied in order to provide the right answers. Where the existing research results are inconclusive this can create ethical problems for the teacher; he naturally wishes to stress the value of sociological research, and if possible to help by summarizing and evaluating its implications, but by doing this he runs the very real risk of creating a premature impression of certainty, and perhaps in the long run bringing sociology into discredit if the solution is found not to work. In addition to this, the choice of a solution for any practical problem requires not merely the perspectives and the factual information that social research can supply, but value judgements about available means and possible outcomes, and assessment of the costs of alternative courses of action. Sociology will be able to help with the assessment of social costs, and may be able to provide information that those making the value judgements regard

6. M. Weber, *The Protestant Ethic and the Spirit of Capitalism* (1958).

as relevant to them; beyond this, the sociologist is no doubt as capable as the next man, but not in his strictly professional capacity. Thus students to whom sociology is being taught so that it may help them in the making of practical decisions need to be made aware of its limitations. Some of these limitations follow from the nature of the discipline; others only hold at a particular stage in its development, and will be overcome when further research has been done or a better theory worked out. If the nature of the disciplinary limitations is understood, sociology will not be expected to provide a magical panacea, nor will its failure to do so lead to disillusion. If the likelihood of new developments is recognized, the initial acquaintance with sociology will run less risk of becoming increasingly out of date. For this risk to be averted, it is necessary to be able to evaluate other people's research even if one does not undertake any of one's own. Without these kinds of understanding, no sociology will be of much use.

Thus the fact that non-specialist students are likely to come to sociology with motives and interests that lead them either to expect too much of it, or to take too little from it, means that they need to be taught in some ways as though they were to become specialists. If they have no acquaintance with general theory, it will be hard for them to apply what they have learnt to new situations. If they are not enabled to make critical judgements of research work, they will be learning by rote in the first place, and what they have learnt will be of dubious value or become increasingly out of date. If they do not learn, from their sociology teaching or from other sources, how to distinguish between value judgements and statements of fact,[7] their sociological understanding is likely to be limited by their own values or those of their teachers.

What kind of course, then, can be devised to satisfy both the sociologist's conception of his subject and the different

7. I am well aware that there are philosophical and practical problems in making this distinction so sharply, but it does not seem profitable to discuss them here.

kinds of students' needs? The time available is usually short, so it must be fairly concise. Numbers of possibilities have been tried, and we shall start by reviewing them and discussing the strengths and weaknesses of each.

THE GENERAL INTRODUCTION TO SOCIOLOGY

This sort of course may vary somewhat in form, but its crucial characteristic is that it is devised as an introduction to the subject for students who subsequently will specialize in sociology, while the non-specialists who take it will not go on any further. This has obvious attractions for the teacher if he has already prepared such a course, or has to give it in any case. Whether or not it is suitable to the needs of non-specialists will depend on its nature. At an introductory level, all students are in one sense equally non-specialists; but those who plan to specialize in the subject are likely to be more strongly motivated to persist even with currently boring work, apart from the greater likelihood that for them the course may take on a value retrospectively that it did not obviously possess at the time. If other students are taking the course simply as part of a liberal education, there may be no particular need to adapt it for their benefit; that is, the wise teacher will have gone to some trouble in any case to ensure that he touches on themes generally found interesting, and that the course is fairly self-sufficient. If, however, the other students are being required to take the course for some more limited purpose, or their own interests are confined to their main subjects, they are unlikely to benefit from a course that makes no deliberate provision for them even if it is relatively complete in itself. The course may be highly relevant to their interests, but such relevance is often not at all evident to the novice; the connexions must be pointed out, and the examples drawn from the right sources, if he is to profit.

'THIS IS SOCIOLOGY'

A course designed for the non-specialist, which aims to cover the whole field of sociology in the time available.

SOCIOLOGY

Courses quite often have names that suggest such an ambitious undertaking, but on closer investigation they will be found not to attempt it. In this case they are only open to the criticism that the students, and perhaps also the teacher, may be led to believe that they have covered sociology. I have not actually come across a course which seriously attempts it, but I have met an academic historian who suggested that such a course would be suitable for his students. When the assumptions implied were pointed out to him he humbly withdrew the suggestion made in unthinking disciplinary arrogance.

SELECTED TITBITS

In this kind of course, appetites are whetted by starting with spicy applications to fields of interest like religion or sexual behaviour (for the general education course) or, say, the behaviour of engineers (for the course for engineers). Later, it is planned to go on to make the broad theoretical points, and to fill in the detailed evidence and the means by which it has been collected. The intention behind such a course is clearly good, since it is planned to show students that sociology can be interesting to anyone and thus to motivate them to pursue it further. The danger is that the more general points will never get made, or that when they do their import will not be appreciated. It can be a rather cynical solution to the problem, in that it may keep the students happy without doing anything serious to further their education. On the other hand it can be no solution at all, in that some students are likely to see that it is being treated in an essentially frivolous way, and are likely to judge sociology accordingly.

SOCIOLOGY OF x

For x substitute art, industry, literature, medicine, etc. as appropriate. Such courses are frequently provided for students who are already involved in the non-sociological study of the same subjects. Thus they will have a strong motive for interest in them, unless they are regarded as a distraction from the serious work on the main subject. (I remember a university English student who was unable to accept that social research could in any sense contribute to knowledge of social reality; for her only literature had this function. I shudder to imagine her reaction to the sociology of literature.) But the main difficulty here is that of teaching the sociology of x without teaching just plain sociology; as in the Selected Titbits course, the student's predispositions may lead him to notice only those parts that fit in with or throw light on his existing ideas, and thus he may never discover what a distinctively sociological approach has to offer. That is, he may pick up the sociological ideas about his subject that he reads or hears, but they will not become organized in his mind in such a way that he can look sociologically at a new problem in the field. Thus there will be some benefit, especially for the bright student who can extrapolate for himself, but it is likely to be rather limited. Industrial sociology, a recognized specialism within the subject, seems to be suffering from this sort of effect at present. It is an area to which many researchers are drawn who do not have formal sociological training, and many courses are offered under such rubrics as 'industrial relations' which do not include any general sociology; the result is that the field no longer has much connexion with general sociology, and both sides are the losers.

PARTICIPATION IN RESEARCH

This kind of course aims to involve the student directly in sociological research, either an *ad hoc* project or one that is taking place in any case. Obviously a main aim is to familiarize the participants with the nature of the research process and the decisions it entails, and by this means to help them to judge the results gained by others and perhaps to carry out research themselves in future.

There are very practical difficulties in arranging such

research participation. If an *ad hoc* project is devised, its character will have to be strongly influenced by the amount of time and resources at the disposal of the class, by their likely capacities, and by the particular kinds of experience that it is thought most valuable to provide; not many ordinary projects, for example, will fit conveniently into ten weeks, require no skills that cannot be taught in three weeks, and offer equally responsible opportunities to twenty people at each stage. If, on the other hand, students are to take part in ongoing research, it is likely that the significant decisions about it will already have been made, that they will not be able to see it through from start to finish, and that they will only be able really to participate in the more humdrum and routine parts of the work. Thus their learning will be limited, and probably their interest too. If this is not to happen, the smooth working of permanent research staff must be considerably disrupted in order to adapt to student needs, and the level of work done by students may be below that which would normally be expected of paid and fully-trained staff. This may provide a happy solution for the absence of a research grant, but it is not a truly satisfactory one, quite apart from the possible element of exploitation.

In addition to these practical difficulties, which may be overcome, there are more fundamental ones. It is of very little value to be acquainted with research methods without some substantive knowledge, and without knowledge of the theoretical considerations that direct the choice of research topics and make some methods appropriate to some topics and other methods to others. If participation in one research project is to be the major learning experience, the student is likely only to become aware of the range of problems raised by that project, and to learn only the techniques used in it, especially if he has not himself had any responsibility for choosing the techniques. If the student is to make choices, the instructor will probably feel that in a limited time he cannot be allowed to make seriously wrong ones and learn by their consequences, and so the element of experience will be reduced. Even if more time is available there are some choices which would be ethically unacceptable, and so they must be ruled out; clumsy interviewing can not only be hurtful to the respondents, but arouse so much hostility that difficulties are created for other researchers for years to come. All these points apply both to the *ad hoc* and to the ongoing project, but there is a further one which is specific to the former: it is not easy for inexperienced students to devise, or for anyone to carry out in a short time, a piece of research that is of serious value to the discipline, and it seems to me both irresponsible in itself and miseducational to carry out research for research's sake. The idea is only too prevalent already that any piece of descriptive research is useful, and I have known a group of university students decide that they want to do a survey and then try to think what it could be of. (When such surveys are done, it generally turns out that the results are unanalysable because the questions were not planned to relate to each other, while questions that would have helped to make a meaningful interpretation of the others were never asked.) 'Research' of this nature is unlikely to have any connexion with sociology, and certainly does not provide an ideal model; proper research is carried out in order to contribute to the development of theory, or to find out social facts relevant to a specific problem, and students will receive a false impression of the function of research if the method by which they are taught implies otherwise.

Thus the method of research participation has considerable difficulties, despite its obvious advantages, and is probably inadvisable by itself, although in conjunction with other methods it could be very successful.

PARTICIPATION IN 'LIFE'

'Life' in practice usually seems to mean social work, or at least the life of socially disadvantaged groups. The idea is presumably that the student will find out How The Other Half Really Lives, and that from this experience some sort of conclusions will follow. It probably is educational to be forced to realize that other people are significantly different from oneself, but that is only a very small step in the direction of social science. The requirement that they should be socially disadvantaged must stem from the confusion between sociology and social work (or even socialism?). To study 'real life' in a sociological way is likely to be more instructive when it is that section of real life with which one is in any case familiar. There is some danger of sociology coming to be regarded as the study only of people different from oneself; certainly some middle-class students already have the impression, culled rather unfairly from the well-known work of the Institute of Community Studies,[8] that sociology is the study of the working class.

CASE STUDIES

Selected pieces of published work are studied. The principles of selection are likely to be at least twofold, works being chosen because they both correspond to the students' interests or needs, and provide good examples of sociological theory and research methods. (A good example is not, of course, always an example of the good.) The main potential disadvantage of this method is again that the general may become lost in the particular, but this can rather easily be counteracted by the manner in which the teaching is done. To begin with, the simple fact of studying more than one case makes comparisons inevitable. Secondly, collateral reading can be set which provides comparative material or discusses the points raised in more general terms. Thirdly, it depends on the teacher's whole approach; questions can be raised at every stage of discussion about why the choice was made of one strategy rather than another, whether the same choice would be made under other circumstances, and whether with hindsight the choice appears to have been a wise one.

8. For instance: M. Young and P. Willmott, *Family and Kinship in East London* (1957); P. Townsend, *The Family Life of Old People*, (1957).

The advantages of the method are manifold. It has the pedagogical advantage of ensuring that concrete examples are always available, and moreover that all the students are likely to be equally familiar with them. It makes it possible to be highly selective within the literature, so that students may become familiar with the best standards of practice and develop norms with which to compare other work, without encouraging an uncritical spirit or glossing over the difficulties of research. But perhaps the most important benefit of this approach is that, if the cases studied are well chosen, it allows the student to see the sociological enterprise as a whole rather than as a set of disconnected parts where theory is studied one week and methods the next and never the twain shall meet. Although this method alone cannot provide familiarity with a wide range of substantive data, it can certainly lead on very well to more extensive reading; I would argue in any case that for the non-specialist, even the vocationally interested non-specialist, to learn a lot of facts is by itself not very useful. However, to the extent that students' interests and the purposes of the course are limited the cases studied can be chosen to express these interests and purposes.

This, therefore, is the method that I would advocate as most likely to be effective, since it combines most of the good points of its alternatives with few of their disadvantages. It can give a real sense of what sociology is like, without improbable pretensions to complete coverage; it can be treated either as an introductory or as an only course; it can focus on special areas of interest, without ignoring the more general considerations; it can provide a sort of vicarious research experience, without the narrowness or practical difficulties of real research participation. (Or it could well be supplemented by research participation.)

Like any other teaching method, however, the case study method can be ineffective. In order to make clearer what I have in mind I shall suggest the principles on which cases should be chosen, and go on to give an example of how they could be treated.

The ideal case would have at least several of these characteristics:

(a) A detailed description of the methods used, and hopefully also of rejected alternatives. (But it can be useful to look at books which give inadequate accounts, in order to show how this makes it difficult to judge the value of their conclusions.)

(b) More than one type of research method used, in particular both quantitative and non-quantitative methods.

(c) The same subject to have been studied by other writers using different methods, and/or the same method to have been used on rather different subjects.

(d) A theoretical background to the research to exist and be made explicit, and the conclusions reached related to it. (But for comparative purposes it can be useful to look at a theoretical research and discuss its relative generalizability.)

(e) To be generally regarded as a fairly important book in its field, so that it merits close study and is more likely to have had commentaries written on it by other authors.

(*f*) To be written in a readable style, with illustrative anecdotes and quotations and clearly presented tables.

A very suitable case, which meets almost all these criteria, is *Union Democracy*.[9] This is a substantial empirical monograph, which is on a subject of fairly general interest and also has broader implications; the atypical existence of 'democracy' within a printers' trade union is discussed in ways which throw light on the preconditions of democratic participation in general and within bureaucratic organizations, and the discussion is related both to past work on the subject and to general sociological theory. The analysis of the data is generally regarded as exemplary for its thoroughness and imagination, especially in the famous section on printers' friendships.

A useful place to start to study the book would be a consideration of the professional and personal reasons for which a sociologist undertakes a piece of research at a par-

9. S. M. Lipset, M. A. Trow and J. S. Coleman, *Union Democracy* (1956).

ticular time and place; in this case one of the authors has given his own detailed account,[10] so personal factors can be discussed less speculatively than usual, and the subject has an obvious political relevance which suggests a simple application of the sociology of knowledge. Possible elements of autobiography in social science could be discussed and exemplified further, and the strengths and weaknesses it lends evaluated, perhaps in comparison with novels. This could lead on to an analysis of the value judgements implicit in the choice of the subject and the way in which it is treated, and such questions as 'Can there be value-neutral social science?', 'How would someone with different values have done the same research?' be raised. Obvious comparisons here are with other books on similar subjects, such as those of Allen and of Goldstein,[11] which could also be used to bring out other points.

The issue of values inevitably draws one's attention to the way in which 'democracy' is defined in different books, and some students might think certain definitions inappropriate or question-begging. This leads to the whole problem of devising adequate operational definitions for complex concepts, and the consequences that the choice of an operational definition has for the final results. Students might investigate other operational definitions – 'family', 'suicide', 'social integration' – and try their own hand at a few. This opens up the whole field of measurement and its assumptions in the social and indeed the physical sciences, and for good students could be followed into the philosophy of science. ('Union Democracy' gives a useful list in an appendix of all the indices used in the text.) Once on the subject of methods, there are many other topics which could be covered: how are interview data used? How are historical data used and related to the interview data? Are the conclusions drawn justified by the data, and if not, what kinds

10. P. E. Hammond, *Sociologists at Work* (1964): S. M. Lipset, 'The Biography of a Research Project: Union Democracy'.
11. V. L. Allen, *Power in Trade Unions* (1954); J. Goldstein, *The Government of British Trade Unions* (1952).

of data would be needed to support them? What is the logic of the study of a single atypical case in order to establish generalizations, and how does this differ from the more usual procedure? How can generalizing from samples ever be justified? Can causation be demonstrated, or legitimately inferred, and if so what kinds of evidence are necessary? and so on.

These methodological topics are closely related to a series of substantive ones. Is the procedure of relating the characteristics of individual printers to the composition of the union chapels to which they belong merely a methodological device, or does it rest on some social reality? This question can be used to consider the relationships between individuals and groups in general (and between psychology and sociology) from the large literature on the subject, perhaps leading on to a comparison of field and laboratory research. The issue of generalization suggests a study of the way in which Lipset and his colleagues have used and modified Michels's[12] initial sweeping generalizations, and the ways in which their new generalizations in turn have been, or could be, used by other authors; what kinds of organizations are similar in relevant respects to the International Typographical Union? Are the results applicable only to other unions, or could they perhaps also tell us something about tennis clubs or hospitals? This implies a general discussion of formal organizations and of class structure which could lead to direct study of either, or perhaps of theoretical ideas such as those of Dahrendorf.[13] This list of suggestions could be extended, but I hope that it is sufficient as it stands to establish the point that a single case study can be used to raise a large number of important issues, which may be chosen and followed up in more or less detail as the teacher thinks fit.

In conclusion, however, I should like to emphasize that my concern here has been with the teaching of sociology,

12. R. Michels, *Political Parties* (1959).
13. R. Dahrendorf, *Class and Class Conflict in an Industrial Society* (1959).

and not with everything that sociologists might reasonably teach. (Although I believe that the case study method advocated is also extremely suitable for teaching other than pure sociology.) Sociology, like other academic disciplines, abstracts from the total social reality. If the aim is to solve real social problems, or to teach students to do so, other disciplines too will be relevant, and an inter-disciplinary approach will be the most appropriate. Interdisciplinary work has its own special problems, which cannot be considered here.[14]

14. For a very valuable discussion, see M. Gluckman and E. Devons (eds.), *Closed Systems and Open Minds* (1964).

Mathematics

ALAN TAYLER, ALAN TAMMADGE,
and PHILIP PRESCOTT

It is becoming commonplace to read in the reports of statements of distinguished industrialists and politicians that the way to make Britain's economy flourish is to stage a technological revolution, and that one of the necessary ingredients is a new generation of mathematically educated managers, planners and directors. The Dainton Report has proposed that all sixth-form students should be required to take mathematics courses to 'A' level. However, the report has not been received without criticism, and it seems unlikely that its proposals will be adopted in the near future. Meanwhile the present situation is almost the reverse of that desired. The majority of our administrators not only finished their mathematical education at sixteen but probably have little idea of what mathematics is about, dismissing it, at least sub-consciously if not openly, as boring sums or impractical abstractions. Nor are they likely to comprehend the revolution in mathematics which the arrival of the computer has instigated.

What then is mathematics about, and what can it do? It is a language – and language is more that just a means of communication, it is a vehicle for thought. No real thought is possible without a language, and with a rich and varied language both clear thinking and accurate communication of ideas are easier to accomplish than with a poor and primitive one. In mathematics, as in a language, each element and rule of operation has to be defined very clearly in order to obtain precise understanding. Such definitions are called axioms. A discussion that can be reduced to mathematical language is removed from the area of prejudice and personal idiosyncrasy and can be carried on objectively. In everyday speech this may not always be the case. For example, it has been shown that there can be significant variation in the understanding by students of a passage in a medical textbook containing the word 'normal'. The word 'normal' can, however, be given a precise meaning in a statistical context.

From the basic elements or axioms logical deduction leads to a mathematical structure, analogous in some ways to a language grammar. Thought and reasoning can be telescoped by the easy use of and familiarity with mathematical structure, and much of this extremely valuable telescopic effect is built into the notation used to describe the structure. The idea of using a very simple representation of a complicated thought has been highly developed in mathematics and is one of its fundamental characteristics. For example, the statement 'The product of the number of terms with the sum of the first term with one half of the product of the common difference and the number of terms diminished by one' is the well-known rule for finding the sum of an arithmetic progression. It needs careful reading before its meaning is apparent, and even then it is not entirely unambiguous. Written in mathematical notation $S = n\{a + \frac{1}{2}(n - 1)d\}$ the meaning is clearly revealed and so is the best way of calculating it, provided that it is understood that the letters represent numbers and that the symbols $+$, $-$, $(\,)$ and $\{\,\}$ represent certain well-known operations on numbers.

Any such representation must be clearly defined so that no ambiguity can arise in the interpretation of the notation. In elementary arithmetic two times three times four is unambiguous, whereas two divided by three divided by four is not. The notation used for division must show which division operation is to be performed first.

As well as possessing structure mathematics has its descriptive writing. Just as a writer uses language in an attempt to recreate or represent a real or human situation, so a mathematician can model or represent real problems. Many problems or situations in everyday life can be modelled so that a mathematical question is posed. As in good writing, considerable skill may be necessary in order to pose a simple enough question which nevertheless includes all the features of importance.

The power and usefulness of mathematics can be easily illustrated by examples, and we will give some later. This aspect alone would justify a general course in mathematics for undergraduate students of all disciplines. A mathematical analysis can and should be one of the standard procedures used in organization and planning. The detailed analysis may be performed by a specialist, but any administrator should be able to discuss with the mathematician certain aspects of the problem. First of all he must have some idea which of his problems might be put in mathematical terms – and this does not imply that they must necessarily be numerical problems. He must be able to understand the mathematician's attempt to model the problem and be able to discuss the assumptions of the model. Finally he must be able to understand and interpret the solution even if it is presented in mathematical form. All this will require that he has some general education in mathematics. For example, many organizations are equipped with computers. The computer can only answer questions put to it by the programmer and its answers will only be as valuable as the questions asked. It is easy for a manager to be persuaded by vast amounts of numerical data, but it is vital that he understands and approves of the assumptions necessary to obtain the data.

Mathematics as a subject seriously studied is, however, much more than a collection of useful techniques. It is a discipline almost exclusively concerned with pattern. A mathematical structure is an attempt to order and codify sequences of patterns of both objects and operations. Most intellectual disciplines are in part a search for pattern among diverse pieces of information. Similarly many management or planning problems involve the construction of a pattern of operation of a complicated organization. This experience of comprehending pattern forms a valuable part of education, and mathematics is probably the best vehicle for obtaining this experience. The necessity for ordered thinking is apparent in mathematics at a very early stage, so that complicated information can be reduced to simple patterns or structures.

Finally there is the intellectual and aesthetic appeal of the subject and the fascination of deep structural problems. There is much to be discovered rather than learnt, and a student can be doing original and creative work early in his studies. It is always possible that a schoolboy may present his master with an improved proof of a theorem of Euclid; and it is quite probable that he may think of a novel application. Good mathematics should have a certain natural simplicity and be the starting point of several avenues of thought. It is very difficult to describe the aesthetic pleasure of good mathematics, but we hope it would be possible to give some taste of it before the end of a general course.

We now consider how a general course might be devised to illuminate all these aspects of mathematics, namely the power and usefulness, the structure and recognition of pattern, and the intellectual and aesthetic appeal.

The course would fall naturally into three parts. First and very important, a clearly presented introduction, in which all the arguments given here as to why mathematics is worth studying are discussed in detail. It must be shown to be relevant to the everyday life of every member of the course, since without great effort and enthusiasm on the part of each student the course must inevitably fail. The second part would consist of a considerable number of fairly elementary mathematical ideas, which would be familiar to most students but would be illustrated by novel applications. The intention would be to demonstrate the power and usefulness of mathematics and give a firm base for the third part of the course. This would consist of a selection of some of the more sophisticated ideas which a specialist undergraduate reading mathematics would meet. The object would be to construct at least one abstract mathematical structure and to attempt to demonstrate the intellectual interest in what the mathematician actually tries to do.

MATHEMATICS

The traditional presentation of mathematics has been to insist on extensive practice with examples in order to obtain familiarity with the language before expecting a full understanding of the ideas. Thus children may spend several years practising elementary multiplication and division without being taught the ideas behind these operations. Whitehead remarks that civilization advances by extending the number of important operations which can be performed without thinking about them, and this philosophy has been taken to justify the traditional approach to mathematical teaching. But to arrive at very interesting and powerful ideas by the traditional method would take a long time. If this approach were used in the general course outlined above it would not be possible in the time available to attempt the third part. One could not omit some of the more elementary sections in order to start the third part earlier, since all the elementary ideas would be needed before the more advanced ideas could be presented. In this respect mathematics is different from many other disciplines in that it is a linear progression of thought.

What then would be the principles on which such a course would be based? It would have to be a course in which the student discovers by himself some mathematical results. They should not be presented to him just to be learnt, since the personal discovery of a mathematical truth is a vivid experience unlikely to be forgotten. The understanding would come through the student's own attempts, with tutorial guidance, to answer carefully posed problems. The solution of each problem would lead on to the next mathematical idea and give the background to the next problem. The structure would be discovered by problem solving, and in this way it should be possible to introduce more difficult ideas reasonably quickly. It will require a high degree of concentrated thought and effort on the part of the student, but his increased maturity compared to the schoolboy should enable him to make these big jumps in comprehension. The problems in the elementary section should be real ones, as relevant as possible to his experience; much of mathematical structure was first discovered in attempts to solve real problems. The principle is to guide but not lead the student along some of the more successful and important avenues of mathematical thought.

A basic course for non-specialist students would begin with elementary arithmetic. This would, however, be presented in a fundamental and analytical way, with emphasis on the ideas rather than the techniques. The rules governing use of the elementary operations of addition, subtraction, multiplication and division would be formalized so that arithmetic can be defined from axioms. Later in the course, for example when matrices are discussed, new arithmetics based on different axioms will be met.

At the same time it will be necessary to look at the basis of arithmetical notation. It is only necessary to compare multiplying 15 by 17 in our (Arabic) numeration system with multiplying XV by XVII in the Roman system to see the great calculating advantage given by the positional notation. It would probably be a good idea to begin by doing some work in a duo-decimal rather than a decimal system. Here two new symbols have to be invented, forcing an awareness of the meaning of our present ten numerals.

The second of our building bricks from which much of the course will develop is the idea of a set. The use of sets and set notation clarifies and gives precision. For example, consider the equation $2x + 3y = 5$. A schoolboy will probably say that this has no solution. What he means is that he cannot find a unique solution. It is easy to see that $x = 1, y = 1$ is a possible solution satisfying the equation. There are, however, many others, for example $x = 2, y = \frac{1}{3}$ or $x = 2\frac{1}{2}$, $y = 0$. In fact this equation has a solution set with an infinite number of members. In linear programming, discussed later, we shall be concerned less with equations than with inequations or inequalities when the solution is almost certainly not unique. Usually there will be a set of solutions, and the problem may well be to choose the best from a number of solutions rather than to obtain any one solution. A simple discussion of sets, and some set notation, should help to clarify this sort of issue.

MATHEMATICS

The next fundamental idea which would have to be discussed in this basic part of the course is the idea of a relation. This comprises in its most simple form merely a set of pairs of objects, not necessarily mathematical. For example, the first element of a pair might be a car and the second element its registration number. There would be a relation between the two objects. A particular registration number would 'map on to' a particular car and vice versa. Another example would be a man's Christian name and the number of letters in that name. Thus the name James 'maps on to' 5. However, the number 5 can map on to many names other than James. Whereas the first example was a one–one relation, i.e. one car determines one registration number and vice versa, this latter example is a many–one relation, i.e. many names map on to the same number of letters. It is easy to construct examples of other types, for example a many–many relation.

When the relation is between mathematical quantities the situation may be different. For example, the sequence of pairs (1, 1), (2, 4), (3, 9) etc. is clearly generated in a special way. It is not necessary to write many of them on paper in order to discover that the second element is being formed by multiplying the first element by itself. There is a rule for deducing the second element when the first is given; whereas there is no rule for connecting a car with its registration number.

A relation is the most general idea in the whole of mathematics and it is used in every application. A relation is implicit in a multiplication table where two numbers map on to one number called their product. Similarly a rectangle is related to a number called its area. Many pairs of numbers have the same product and many rectangles have the same area, so that these are examples of many–one relations. A valuable example of a one–one relation is that a point in a plane is related to a pair of numbers called its co-ordinates. This idea is extensively used and enables one to make a drawing on paper to illustrate many of the statements in algebra. Such a drawing is called a graph. Graphs are also used to represent relationships given in terms of numerical data, and we shall give examples of this later.

The collection, analysis and interpretation of numerical data forms the part of mathematics called statistics. The hardest operation is usually the interpretation of the data, which involves ideas of probability. An impossible event is said to have probability 0 and a certain one, probability 1. Between these two extremes the probability of an event occurring is given a measure consisting of a number between 0 and 1. The probability of an event occurring may be found either theoretically or experimentally. For example the probability of a coin, when tossed, coming down with a head uppermost is $\frac{1}{2}$. The probability of throwing a total of 7 with two dice can be found similarly from the ratio of the number of ways of throwing a total of 7 with two dice to the total number of different ways in which two dice can combine. A total of 7 can be obtained as $1 + 6, 2 + 5, 3 + 4, 4 + 3, 5 + 2, 6 + 1$, six ways in all. The number of ways two dice can land is six times six, thirty-six ways in all. The probability of a total of 7 is, therefore, $\frac{6}{36}$ or $\frac{1}{6}$. On the other hand the probability of meeting someone who is aged twenty-one cannot be obtained theoretically. It will be the ratio of the total number of people aged twenty-one to the total population, and may be determined only by reference to a population census. We could have determined an experimental probability for the problem of throwing a total of 7 with two dice. If the dice are thrown ten, then 100, then 1,000 times and the number of times the total is 7 is noted, then the experimental probabilities can be calculated. They should become closer and closer to the theoretical value of $\frac{1}{6}$. Some simple experiments with dice or coins quickly enables a student to discover the following two rules for probability. If an event A has probability a and event B has probability b, then the probability of *either* event A *or* event B occurring is $a + b$. The probability of events A *and* B occurring is $a \times b$ provided always that the two events A and B are quite separate. We shall use these ideas in some examples later.

MATHEMATICS

We next develop the idea of a mathematical relation between numbers. If there is a mapping b of a number t on to another number s, we say that s is a function of t and write $s = b(t)$. A very interesting class of functions are those which are continuous. We cannot until later define this precisely, but the idea is that if the graph of the function were drawn it would consist of a continuous curve. The student should be encouraged to draw graphs of various functions

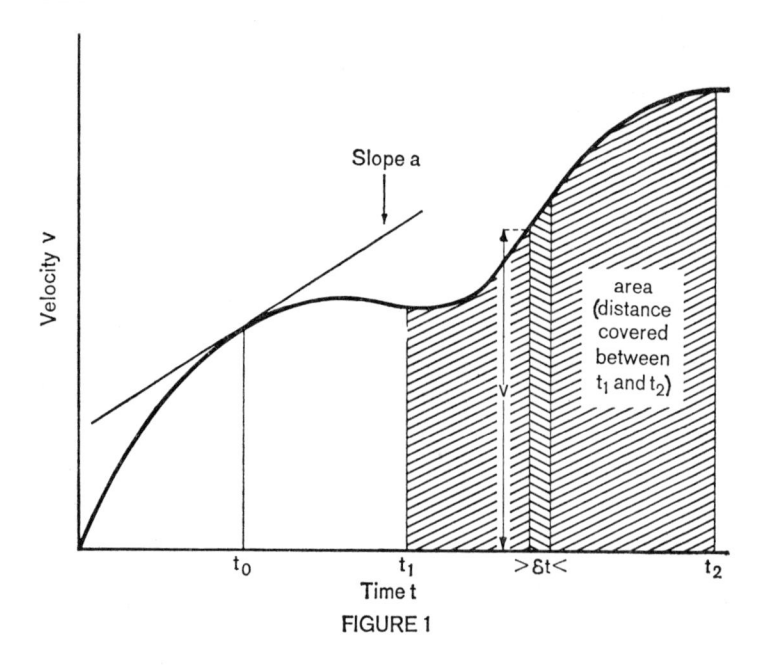

FIGURE 1

and be presented with some examples which are not continuous. He will have no difficulty in drawing tangents to a smooth continuous curve, and this procedure introduces the idea of the slope of a curve at a given point. Consider now that the curve was obtained by plotting the speed v of a car as a function of time t, and suppose that the speed is not constant (Figure 1). What does the slope of the curve at a given time mean? It is the ratio of the change in the speed during a small interval to the time elapsed in that small interval. This is what we mean by the car's acceleration a, and it could be obtained by drawing the tangent at some time t_0 and measuring its slope. We can also ask what does the area under the curve between the given times t_1 and t_2 mean? It can be shown to be the distance travelled between times t_1 and t_2. This is best demonstrated by dividing the range of time t_1 to t_2 into many equal ranges of time δt. In each small time range the velocity is sufficiently nearly constant to justify the statement that the distance travelled is $v\delta t$, that is the area of the rectangle of height v and width δt. The total distance travelled is the sum of all these distances and is therefore the area under the curve. Many other examples can be constructed which demonstrate the value of finding the slope of a curve and the area beneath it.

These ideas of slope and area are, however, rather imprecise and their meaning is not clear if the curve is rapidly varying. A proper mathematical definition is therefore necessary, and this requires the notion of a limit. Suppose one takes a pace along a line, then a half-pace, then a quarter-pace, than an eighth of a pace, and so on. At each step one moves half-way nearer the point which was initially two paces away from the start. It is easy to see from this that the series $1 + \frac{1}{2} + \frac{1}{4} + \frac{1}{8} + \ldots$ will come as near to 2 as we please if we add more and more terms. It is not quite so obvious why the same thing does not happen if one starts with a pace, then a half-pace, then a third of a pace, then a quarter of a pace, and so on. In this case one can in fact progress as far as one likes given enough steps. Thus the sum of the first n terms of the series $1 + \frac{1}{2} + \frac{1}{3} + \frac{1}{4} + \ldots$ can be made greater than any given number provided n is taken to be large enough. We say that the series is divergent or that the sum of its terms has no limit. On the other hand the series $1 + \frac{1}{2} + \frac{1}{4} + \frac{1}{8} \ldots$ is convergent, and the sum of its terms has the limit 2. If we call the sum of its first n terms s_n, then we write $s_n \to 2$ as $n \to \infty$ where the arrow means 'tends to'. The idea of a limit should be amplified by numerous examples, and finally a technical definition could be given.

It will now be possible to give a mathematical definition

of the slope of a graph representing the function $s = b(t)$. It will be the derivative db/dt of the function $b(t)$ with respect to t. This is defined as the limit of the ratio

$$\frac{\text{the change in } b \text{ due to a change in } t}{\text{the corresponding change in } t}$$

as the change in t becomes small or tends to zero. Thus if the velocity of the car in our example is $v = b(t)$, its acceleration will be db/dt. The notation used is to remind the reader that if he thinks of db and dt as small changes in b and t, the ratio db/dt will be an approximate value for the derivative.

At this stage it is probably a good idea to look at several kinds of functions. The first would be the exponential function or the law of growth. This is of fundamental importance since the theoretical behaviour of many natural phenomena is that they grow exponentially with time. For example the world population might be growing exponentially with time, and (to take a more manageable example) cultures of bacteria certainly do so. Suppose that at a certain hour there are b bacteria in a colony and that the number trebles every hour. After one further hour there will be $b \times 3$ bacteria, after another hour $b \times 3^2$ and so on. After t hours there will be $b \times 3^t$ bacteria in the colony. It is easy to see that trebling the number each hour means that the actual increase in any hour is twice the number present at the start of that hour. This is an illustration of the law of growth: the rate of increase of bacteria per hour depends on the number present at the start of the hour. Thought of graphically the rate of increase per hour will be approximately the slope of the curve $b(t)$. Thus in mathematical notation $db/dt = 2b$. This is called a differential equation for b in terms of t. Any differential equation of the form $db/dt = kb$ where k is a number implies that b varies exponentially with t, or that b is an exponential function of t. It also implies that t varies logarithmically with b or that t is a logarithmic function of b. One could explain these properties in terms of relations, as discussed above. Thus it can be easily shown that a logarithmic relation is a mapping from one set of numbers on to another in such a way that a multiplication sum in the first becomes an addition sum in the second. This example shows how a familiar idea can be viewed from a very different standpoint. The techniques of logarithmic calculation will probably be well remembered, but the theory may have been forgotten (or more likely never attempted) by most students.

Finally it would be possible to define an integral as an anti-derivative and prove the fundamental theorem of integral calculus. The theorem, which is rather unexpected, states that it is necessary to use the anti-derivative to find the area beneath a curve. At first sight there would appear little connection between a derivative and the area under the curve. However, in our example of the car, if the distance travelled had been $s(t)$, then its speed $v = b(t)$ would have been ds/dt. Thus to find s, knowing b, requires that the opposite operation of differentiation, i.e. integration, is performed.

All the important ideas of physics, for example, heat, temperature, mass, volume, time, are likely to be related in any practical situation by derivatives and integrals. Solving a heat problem almost certainly means solving a differential equation; that is some equation containing derivatives. This is quite a different proposition from solving an algebraic equation. In an algebraic equation the solution set is a set of values of the variable. In a differential equation the solution is a relation between variables – an algebraic equation in fact. This leads to another idea – that these very algebraic relations or polynomials are themselves elements of an algebra similar to the algebra of numbers which has been studied before. Abstract algebra is the name given to the study of the differences and resemblances of these algebras, and at least one example of a different algebra will be studied later in the course.

Enough has now been said about some of the constituent parts of an elementary course to demonstrate that it does not progress very far beyond the ideas of elementary mathematics but that there are many opportunities for extending

MATHEMATICS

the student into some of the deeper and more fundamental facets of the subject. The method of doing this would be by presenting real problems to the students for them to answer.

The following is a typical series of four examples which might be presented. They arise from the organization of a manufacturing company.

EXAMPLE 1

The first application is called linear programming and follows on the ideas of sets and graphs discussed earlier. Suppose that a company manufactures two products each of which requires the use of three machines for a known number of minutes. The times required for each product and the total times available per day on each machine are summarized in the table below. The times are given in minutes.

		Machines		
		A	B	C
Products	1	5	2	3
	2	2	6	4
Total time available		500	600	440

If the profits on the products are £3 and £2 respectively, how many of each should the company attempt to produce each day so that the total profit is a maximum?

If the numbers of each product to be produced each day are denoted by x and y, the time required on machine A will be given by $(5x + 2y)$ minutes, which must be less than or equal to 500 minutes. This restriction on the values of x and y can be expressed algebraically by the inequality

$$5x + 2y \leq 500.$$

Similarly, using the total times available on the other machines, two further restrictions are imposed. These are

$$2x + 6y \leq 600$$
and
$$3x + 4y \leq 440.$$

Since both x and y are positive, the inequalities $x \geq 0$ and $y \geq 0$ must also hold.

The problem is to determine the values of x and y which, subject to the five restrictions above, maximize the total profit.

The solution to this problem may be found diagrammatically using a graph of y against x. The number of items of the first product, i.e. x, is plotted along the horizontal axis

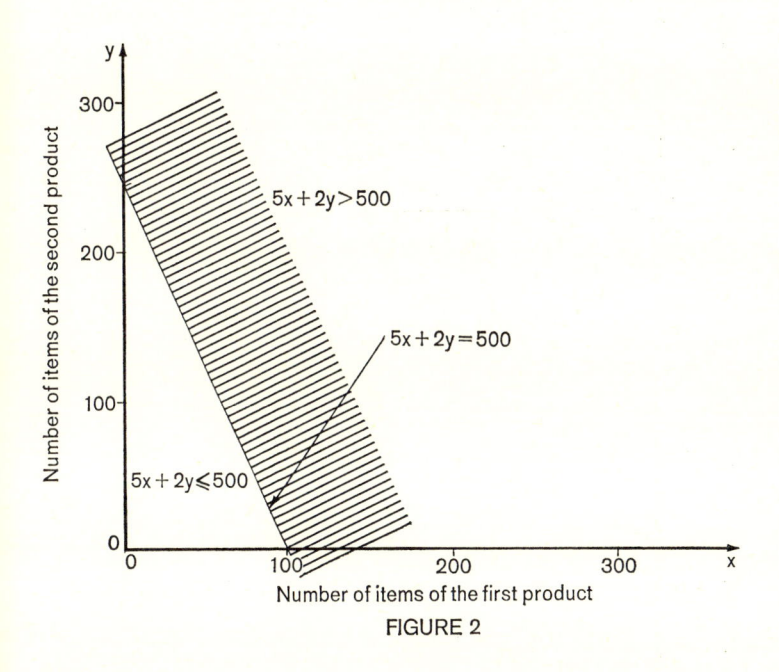

FIGURE 2

and the number of items of the second product, i.e. y, is plotted along the vertical axis. Each of the conditions imposed on the values of x and y may be represented on the graph by a straight line. Points on one side of the line have co-ordinates which satisfy the inequality while points on the other side have co-ordinates which do not. The first inequality $5x + 2y \leq 500$ may be expressed in the form $y \leq -\frac{5}{2}x + 250$. The equation

$$y = -\tfrac{5}{2} x + 250$$

MATHEMATICS

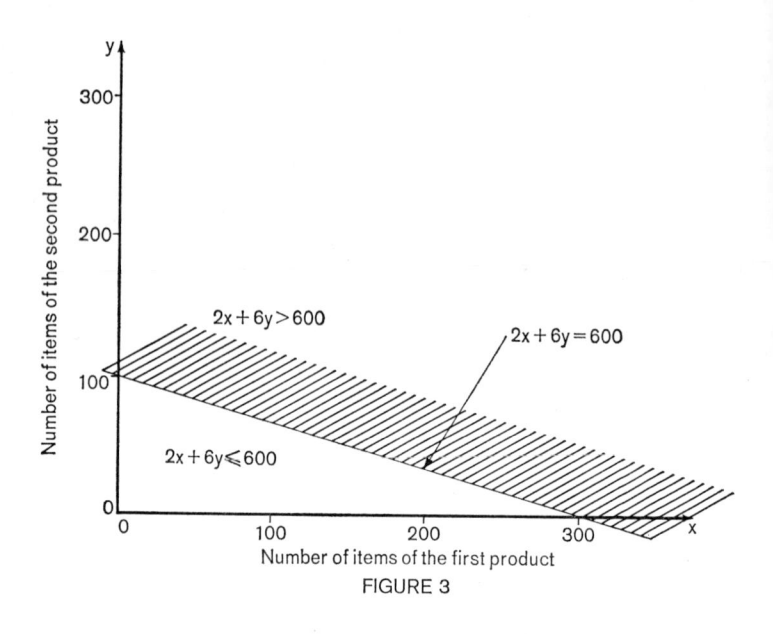

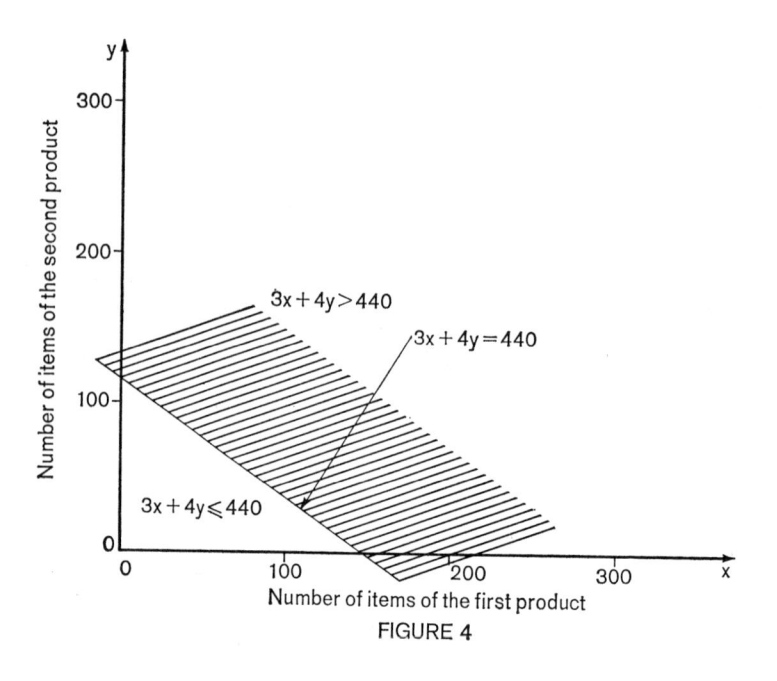

FIGURE 3

FIGURE 4

will be represented by a straight line, with slope $-\frac{5}{2}$, cutting the y axis at the value 250 as shown in Figure 2. The co-ordinates x and y of any point on the unshaded side of the line in Figure 2 satisfy the inequality while those of any point on the shaded side do not.

In the same way regions of points whose co-ordinates satisfy the other inequalities may be represented by the unshaded areas in Figures 3, 4 and 5.

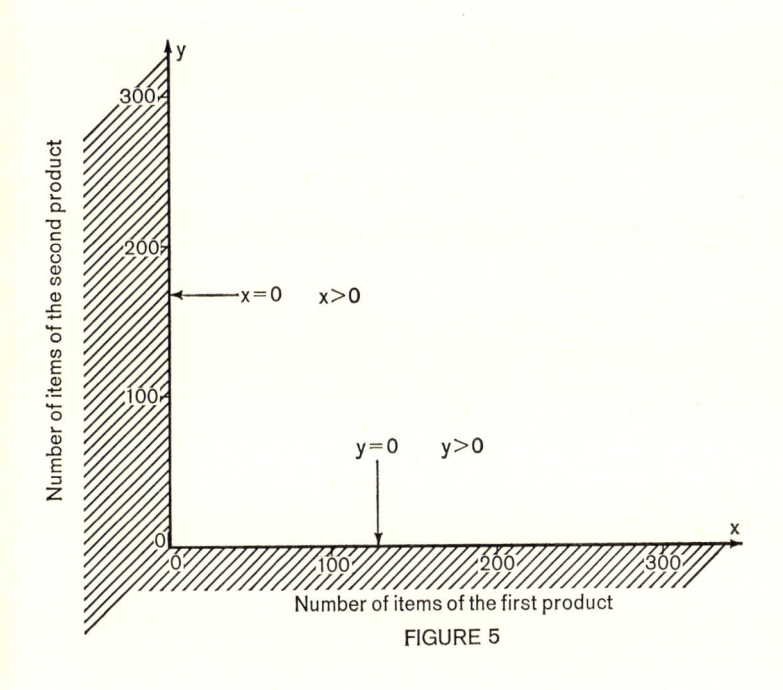

FIGURE 5

When these five graphs are superimposed, as in Figure 6, they determine a region, called the feasible region, consisting of points whose co-ordinates x and y satisfy all the restrictions. It now remains to find the point within the feasible region at which the profit is maximized.

The profit, £P, is given by the equation
$$P = 3x + 2y$$

MATHEMATICS

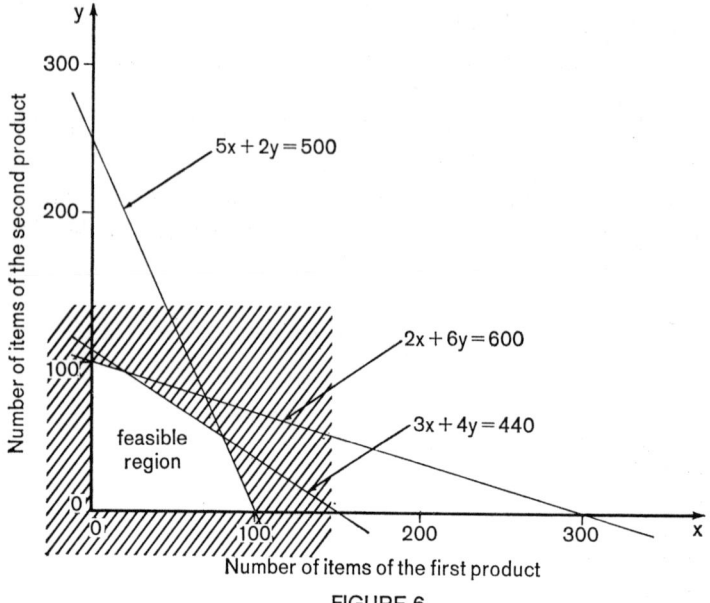

FIGURE 6

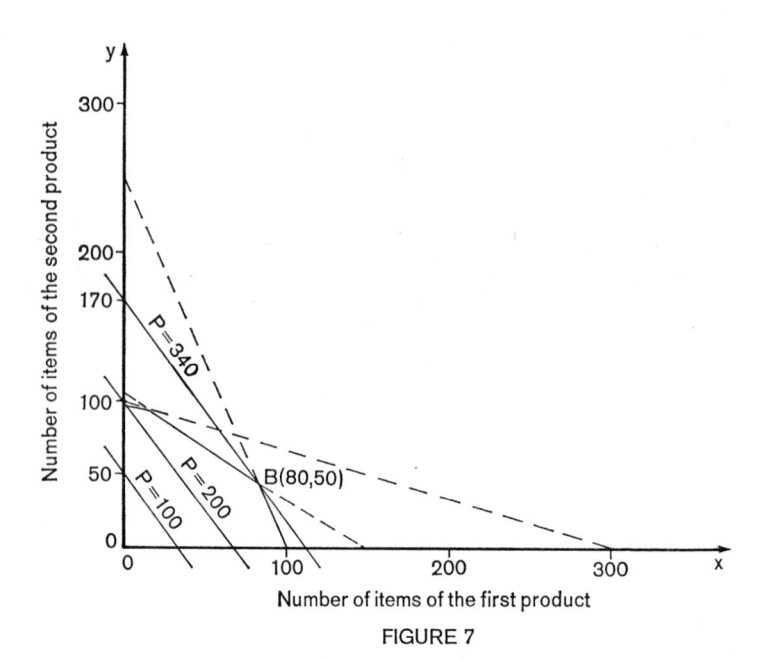

Number of items of the second product (y-axis)
Number of items of the first product (x-axis)

$5x + 2y = 500$
$2x + 6y = 600$
$3x + 4y = 440$

feasible region

FIGURE 7

Number of items of the second product (y-axis)
Number of items of the first product (x-axis)

$P = 100$
$P = 200$
$P = 340$
$B(80, 50)$

which may be written in the form

$$y = -\tfrac{3}{2} x + \tfrac{1}{2}.$$

This is the equation of a straight line with a slope of $-\tfrac{3}{2}$ cutting the y axis at P/2. Figure 7 shows several of these lines for various values of P. Of all the lines with this slope, the one which has the largest intercept P/2 on the y axis, and which intersects the feasible region, is the line through B, the point in the feasible region with co-ordinates $x = 80$ and $y = 50$. This line has an intercept of 170 which corresponds to the value of 340 for P.

The company, therefore, will make the maximum profit of £340 if it manufactures eighty items of the first product and fifty of the second product each day.

Usually linear programming problems which occur in practice involve many restrictions imposed on more than two unknown variables. Graphical methods inevitably restrict us to two-variable problems since there can only be two co-ordinate axes on a plane piece of paper. We shall see later how one might represent n-variable problems in 'n-dimensional geometry'. Techniques have been developed and refined which may be used to solve complex problems of this nature with the aid of high-speed computers.

EXAMPLE 2

The second illustration is an application of probability theory to a queueing problem. Suppose that the company has a large fleet of delivery vehicles and its own servicing facilities capable of servicing one vehicle each day. Vehicles requiring service are brought to the servicing area at the beginning of each day. At the end of the day the vehicle serviced that day is returned to the delivery department. Suppose also that no more than two vehicles are brought in for servicing on any one day, and that on average, in a ten-day period, there are three days on which no vehicles arrive for service, five days when one vehicle arrives and two days when two vehicles arrive. In other words, the experimental

MATHEMATICS

probabilities with which either 0, 1 or 2 vehicles arrive for servicing are $\frac{3}{10}$, $\frac{1}{2}$ and $\frac{1}{5}$ respectively.

If it costs the company £2 for each vehicle out of use for a day, will it be economical to improve the servicing facilities, at an extra cost of £3 a day, so that two vehicles may be serviced instead of one? A decision should be reached by comparing the increase in costs required to improve the facilities with the decrease in costs resulting from having fewer vehicles waiting in the service queue.

The problem is to determine the costs of operating the two servicing facilities. However, since the actual number of vehicles arriving each day for service is not known but only the probability of 0, 1 or 2 vehicles arriving, it is not possible to determine in advance exactly what the costs will be each day. However, probability theory may be used to find how much the costs would be on average over a longer period of time. These average costs, or expected costs as they are more usually called, may be found in the following way.

Let p_n denote the probability that there are n vehicles, including any new arrivals, waiting for service at the beginning of a day. The cost of having n vehicles out of use for a day is £$2n$, and p_n is the probability of incurring the cost of £$2n$. The expected cost is therefore the sum of the products $p_n \times 2n$ for all values of n, i.e.

expected cost = £C = £$(2p_1 + 4p_2 + 6p_3 + \ldots)$.

With the existing facilities, where one vehicle only may be serviced each day, there are two situations which would result in the queue of waiting vehicles being empty on a particular day in the future. Firstly, the queue will be empty if it was empty the day before and no vehicles arrived for service that morning. Secondly it will be empty if it contained one vehicle the day before and no vehicles arrived that morning since that vehicle will have been serviced during the day and returned.

The probability that the queue was empty the day before is p_0, and the probability that no vehicle arrived that morning is $\frac{3}{10}$. Therefore the probability that the queue was empty the day before and no vehicle arrived is $\frac{3}{10}p_0$ by the $a \times b$

rule described earlier. Similarly, as the probability that the queue the day before contained one vehicle is p_1, the probability that the queue the day before contained one vehicle and no vehicle arrived that morning is $\frac{3}{10} p_1$. Since the queue on the day being considered will be empty if either of these two situations occurs, then the $a + b$ rule applies and the probability that the queue is empty is given by

$$p_0 = \tfrac{3}{10} p_0 + \tfrac{3}{10} p_1 .$$

This equation in terms of p_0 and p_1 is the first of a set of equations linking the probabilities $p_0, p_1, p_2, p_3 \ldots$ etc. The remaining equations may be found by similar arguments as follows.

There are three situations which will result in there being one vehicle in the queue on the day under consideration. Either the queue the day before was empty or contained one vehicle, and one arrived that morning, or the queue the day before contained two vehicles and none arrived that morning. The probability that the queue contains one vehicle is found by summing the probabilities for the three situations, giving for the second equation

$$p_1 = \tfrac{1}{2} p_0 + \tfrac{1}{2} p_1 + \tfrac{3}{10} p_2 .$$

In the same way the equations

$$p_2 = \tfrac{1}{5} p_0 + \tfrac{1}{5} p_1 + \tfrac{1}{2} p_2 + \tfrac{3}{10} p_3$$
$$p_3 = \tfrac{1}{5} p_2 + \tfrac{1}{2} p_3 + \tfrac{3}{10} p_4$$
$$p_4 = \tfrac{1}{5} p_3 + \tfrac{1}{2} p_4 + \tfrac{3}{10} p_5$$
$$p_5 = \tfrac{1}{5} p_4 + \tfrac{1}{2} p_5 + \tfrac{3}{10} p_6$$

etc., may be obtained.

The equations for $n \geq 3$ may be rewritten in the general form

$$p_n = \tfrac{1}{5} p_{n-1} + \tfrac{1}{2} p_n + \tfrac{3}{10} p_{n+1}$$

which may be simplified to

$$5p_n = 2p_{n-1} + 3p_{n+1} .$$

The solution of this set of equations, called difference equations, can be verified to be

$$p_n = A + B \left(\tfrac{2}{3}\right)^n, \text{ for } n \geq 2$$

where A and B are constants.

When $p_2 = A + B\left(\frac{2}{3}\right)^2$ is substituted into the equation
$$p_1 = \tfrac{1}{2}p_0 + \tfrac{1}{2}p_1 + \tfrac{3}{10}p_2$$
it is found that $p_0 + p_1 = A + \tfrac{2}{3} B$.

A and B may be found using the fact that, since the number of vehicles in the queue must be either 0 or 1 or 2 or 3 etc., the sum of these probabilities must be 1.

That is $p_0 + p_1 + p_2 + p_3 + \ldots = 1$
i.e. $[A + \tfrac{2}{3} B] + [A + \left(\tfrac{2}{3}\right)^2 B] + [A + \left(\tfrac{2}{3}\right)^3 B] + \ldots = 1$.
Clearly $A = 0$ or else we would have a divergent series $A(1 + 1 + 1 + \ldots)$. Using the fact that the sum of the series $\tfrac{2}{3} + \left(\tfrac{2}{3}\right)^2 + \left(\tfrac{2}{3}\right)^3 + \ldots$ is 2, $B = \tfrac{1}{2}$.

The general solution for $n \geq 2$ is therefore
$$p_n = \tfrac{1}{2}\left(\tfrac{2}{3}\right)^n.$$
p_0 and p_1 may be found by substituting the values of p_2 and p_3 in the original equations and solving the simultaneous equations $p_0 + p_1 = \tfrac{1}{3}$ and $7p_0 = 3p_1$.
These give $p_0 = \tfrac{1}{10}$ and $p_1 = \tfrac{7}{30}$.

The expected cost may now be determined by inserting these probabilities into the expression for C.
$$C = 2p_1 + 4p_2 + 6p_3 + \ldots$$
$$= 2 \cdot \tfrac{7}{30} + 4 \cdot \tfrac{1}{2}\left(\tfrac{2}{3}\right)^2 + 6 \cdot \tfrac{1}{2}\left(\tfrac{2}{3}\right)^3 + \ldots$$
$$= 5 \cdot 8 \text{ (after some calculation)}.$$

The expected cost of operating the present facilities is therefore £5 16s. 0d.

We can much more easily calculate the cost of increasing the facilities. If the facilities are increased so that two vehicles can be serviced each day the system will eventually reach the situation where the queue of vehicles consists of new arrivals only. In that situation the probability of incurring a cost of £2 is $\tfrac{1}{2}$, and the probability of incurring a cost of £4 is $\tfrac{1}{5}$. The expected cost therefore of operating this system, including the extra cost of improving the facilities, is
$$£(3 + 2 \cdot \tfrac{1}{2} + 4 \cdot \tfrac{1}{5}) = £4 \text{ 16s. 0d.}$$

Comparing these costs it can be seen that there will be a saving of £1 a day, on average, if the extra facilities are provided.

EXAMPLE 3

This is another aspect of probability theory.

The company has received the offer of a contract to supply some special components. The buyer has specified that he is prepared to pay £6 each for these components provided that their lengths are not less than 98 millimetres and not greater than 102 millimetres. The company's manufacturing process can be controlled so that the average length of the components is 100 millimetres, but there are random variations and the actual lengths of the components will sometimes be a little more and sometimes a little less. The cost of manufacturing and inspecting each component is £2 and any component which is unacceptable to the buyer is unsaleable. Will it be profitable to accept the contract?

The company's profit on each satisfactory component is £4 and the loss on other components is £2. The company will therefore make a profit on the contract if the manufacturing process is such that the proportion of acceptable components is greater than one-third. There are several ways in which the company can attempt to determine this proportion. The method chosen depends on how much information is available beforehand about the manufacturing process.

intervals in millimetres	number of components with length in these intervals	proportion of total number
94–95	10	0·010
95–96	40	0·040
96–97	60	0·060
97–98	80	0·080
98–99	125	0·125
99–100	180	0·180
100–101	175	0·175
101–102	155	0·155
102–103	95	0·095
103–104	40	0·040
104–105	28	0·028
105–106	12	0·012
	1000	1·000

MATHEMATICS

If the process is similar to one employed in the past, these previous results may be used to form a graph from which the proportion of acceptable components may be estimated. It is constructed by dividing the range of possible lengths into small intervals and recording, for each interval, the number of components whose lengths lie in this interval. The above table shows the results for 1,000 components recorded sequentially.

The third column in the table gives the proportion of the total number of components in each interval.

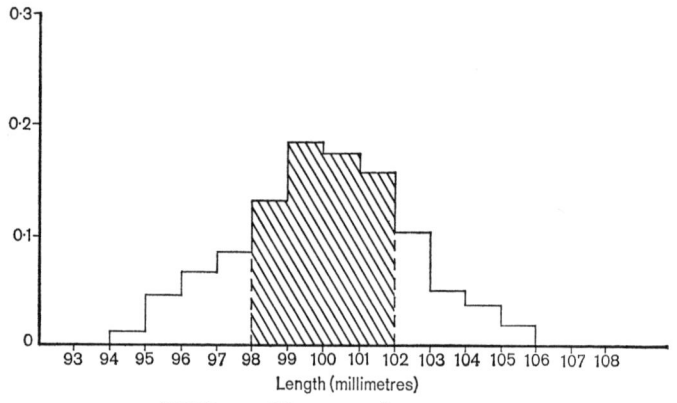

FIGURE 8 Histogram of Tabulated Data

Figure 8 shows how the graph is constructed from this table. A block, with area corresponding to the proportion given in the third column, is drawn above each interval. The shaded area of the graph (which is called a histogram) represents the proportion of components with lengths falling within the limits specified by the buyer. Here this proportion is $0 \cdot 635$. Provided the process to be used to manufacture the special components gives rise to the same form of distribution of lengths as in the table the company can be sure of making a handsome profit on the contract.

Very often, however, detailed information of this kind is not available and a theoretical distribution of the lengths of the components has to be postulated and tested. The Normal Distribution is the most important of these theoretical distributions and is shown in Figure 9. (This is a precise use of the word Normal since the equation of such a curve is precisely known.) Provided that the cost of setting up the manufacturing process is not prohibitive the company could arrange to produce a small number of these special components so that the assumption that the lengths will be Normally distributed may be tested using statistical procedures. Tables are available of the area under the Normal

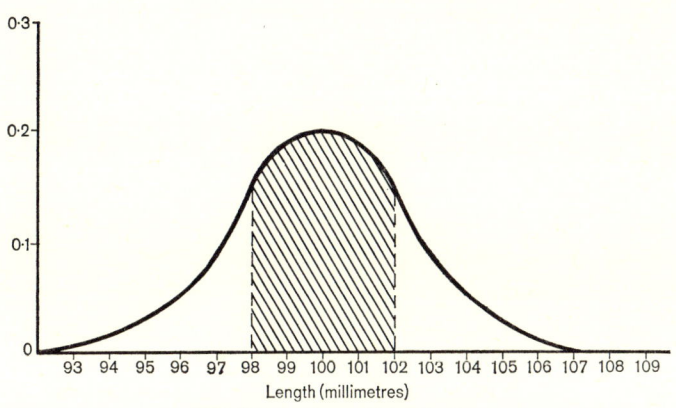

FIGURE 9 Normal Distribution

curve and may be used to find the shaded area shown in Figure 9. This gives an estimate of the proportion of satisfactory components.

EXAMPLE 4

The final illustration of an application of mathematics concerns advertising policy. It is extremely important for a manufacturer to be able to assess the effect of his competitor's sales and advertising on his own sales, and to be able to determine how much advertising to arrange to maintain or increase his share of the market. Problems of this kind may be tackled by setting up a mathematical model to represent what would happen if certain policies were adopted.

In practice, complicated models involving many variables are used because there are usually many manufacturers competing for a fixed market and their policies are continually being changed. Many companies, realizing how costly it can be to allow their competitors to gain an advantage, carry out simulation procedures on computers to investigate the effects of different advertising policies, hoping to be ready to counteract any change in their competitors' policy with a suitable change in their own.

A very simple model will be used to illustrate how surprising some of these effects can be.

Suppose that the company's sales during week n are denoted by x_n and their competitor's sales by y_n, so that the starting sales are x_0 and y_0, in the first week the sales are x_1 and y_1, in the second week x_2 and y_2, and so on. Suppose also that both products are good so that the previous week's sales have a beneficial effect on this week's sales for each company and a detrimental effect on each other's sales.

This situation may be represented by the model
$$x_{n+1} = ax_n - by_n + u$$
$$y_{n+1} = -cx_n + dy_n + v$$
where the coefficients a,b,c, and d may be determined from past experience or perhaps from a consumer survey, and u and v are the increases in the sales due to expenditure on advertising. Having obtained values for a,b,c, and d, and knowing approximately the value of v from the intensity of their competitor's advertising campaign, the company can, by investigating the effects of using different values of u in the model, determine how much they need to spend on advertising to increase their share of the market.

Consider the sales curves corresponding to a few hypothetical examples.

Suppose that the products of the two companies are of a similar standard so that $a = d = 1.1$ and $b = c = 0.1$. Suppose also that the sales this week for both companies are equal and that this volume of sales is taken as the unit, i.e.

$x_0 = y_0 = 1$. It has been estimated that the competitor is spending sufficient on advertising to increase his sales by 0.19 units. What will be the effect on the sales if the company were to spend sufficient to increase their sales by 0.20 units?

The model to represent this situation is

$$x_{n+1} = 1.1\, x_n - 0.1\, y_n + 0.20,$$
$$y_{n+1} = -0.1\, x_n + 1.1\, y_n + 0.19.$$

Series of values $x_0, x_1, x_2, \ldots$, and $y_0, y_1, y_2, \ldots$, may be found by successive applications of these equations starting with $x_0 = 1$ and $y_0 = 1$. The first few values are $x_0 = 1$, $x_1 = 1.20$, $x_2 = 1.401$, and $y_0 = 1, y_1 = 1.19, y_2 = 1.379$.

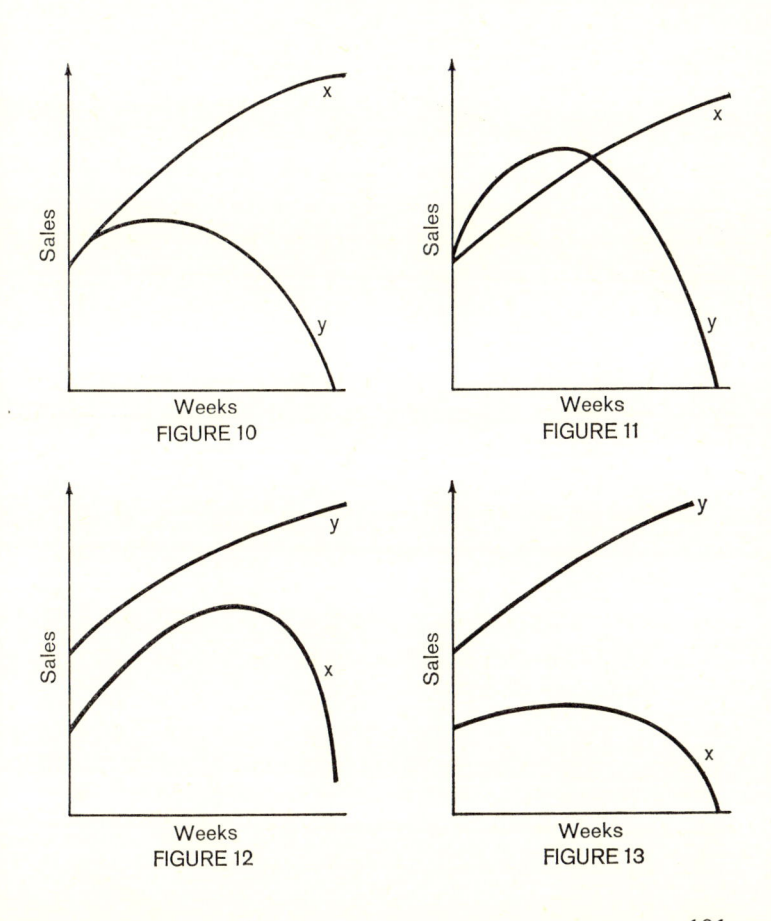

FIGURE 10

FIGURE 11

FIGURE 12

FIGURE 13

MATHEMATICS

Figure 10 shows the sales curves obtained by plotting these two series of values for successive weeks. These show that the difference in advertising, although small, is sufficient to enable the company to capture the entire market if the competitor continues with his present policy.

As a second example where the initial sales are the same consider the model

$$x_{n+1} = 1.2\, x_n - 0.1\, y_n + 0.1,$$
$$y_{n+1} = -0.2\, x_n + 1.1\, y_n + 0.4.$$

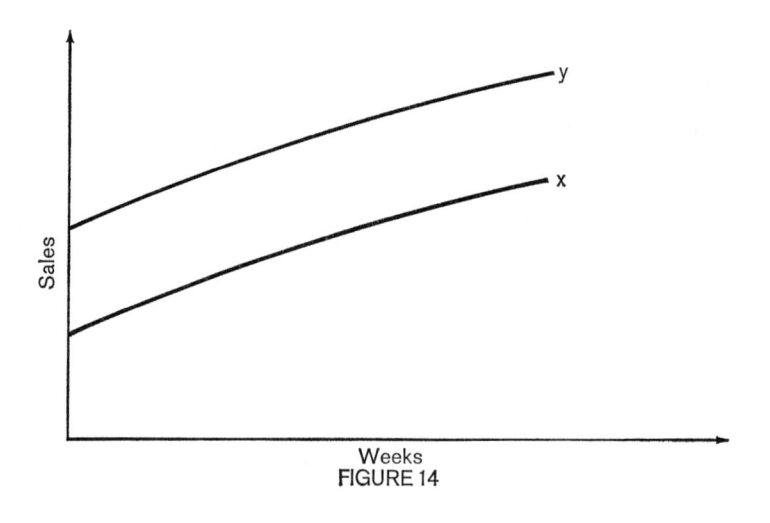

FIGURE 14

This model represents the case where the company's product is slightly better than the competitor's product but the competitor is pursuing a large advertising campaign. The sales curves for this situation are shown in Figure 11. The extra advertising boosts sales initially but is not sufficient to have a lasting effect.

The starting point for these models has a considerable effect on the sales curves, as is indicated in Figures 12 and 13, which use the same models as Figures 10 and 11 except that the competitor's initial sales were larger. Most manufacturers realize the importance of issuing as many free samples as possible when launching a new product in a competitive market.

Figure 14 shows how costly it can be to allow a competitor to get a head start. The model for these sales curves is

$$x_{n+1} = 1.1 x_n - 0.2 y_n + 0.6,$$
$$y_{n+1} = -0.2 x_n + 1.1 y_n + 0.3.$$

Although the products are of the same standard, if the company allows its competitors to start with double the initial sales it will have to achieve twice the advertising effect in order to keep the sales gap constant.

So much, then, for some typical problems. In the final section we wish to return to more abstract concepts in mathematics.

There are many possible mathematical structures which might be presented to a student participating in a general course. One of these structures, that of linear algebra and vector spaces, can, however, be shown to be much the most valuable and relevant. The major reason for its relevance is the arrival of the computer and the advances of computer technology, and one would therefore begin this latter part of the course with a discussion of the powers of a computing machine. It would be desirable to enlarge upon the fundamental notion that computers are machines which are very fast and accurate when presented with simple arithmetic. The mathematical implications of this fundamental property should be carefully discussed, and some practice should be given in actually using a computer to solve one or two straightforward problems. A typical example might be to calculate the numerical values of the variable x for which a given algebraic relation takes the value zero. This is called finding the zeros or roots of a given function. If the given function were $x^2 - c$, where c is a given number greater than zero, then the square root of c will be calculated. A second example is to obtain the solution of a set of simultaneous equations. Suppose that there are three unknown quantities x_1, x_2, and x_3 connected by three relations

$$a_{11}x_1 + a_{12}x_2 + a_{13}x_3 = y_1$$
$$a_{21}x_1 + a_{22}x_2 + a_{23}x_3 = y_2$$
$$a_{31}x_1 + a_{32}x_2 + a_{33}x_3 = y_3$$

where y_1, y_2, y_3 are known numbers. (The symbols a_{11}, a_{12}, a_{13}, a_{21} etc. represent known numbers. The subscripts denote which equation they are in and which unknown they multiply. Thus a_{12} is in the first equation for y_1 and multiplies the second unknown x_2.) Then, in general, a computer can be easily programmed to obtain the values of x_1, x_2 and x_3 which satisfy these relations.

It can also deal with the situation in which there are many more unknowns x_1, x_2 ... x_n and n equations connecting them.

Probably the most important implication is that it is now possible to deal with pieces of information containing a large number of numerical constituents. For example, a collection of numbers such as 1, 2, 15, 3, 12, 0 might represent the entries in a milkman's order book for the first six houses in a street. This collection is called by the mathematician an ordered set and each number in it is called a component. The ordering and number of components are both important parts of the information. To show that it is all one piece of information it is usual to enclose it with brackets, thus (1, 2, 15, 3, 12, 0). It is also important to know to which set of numbers each component belongs: if each entry represents the number of bottles of milk to be delivered then each component belongs to the set of integers (whole numbers). In the computing example above the solution is the ordered set (x_1, x_2, x_3) but the components will now no longer necessarily belong to the set of integers.

These two examples have only six and three components respectively and can be easily written down on paper. An example with one hundred components would, however, be rather clumsy to write down, especially if we wished to mention it several times. This kind of discussion should lead the student to the idea of representing an ordered set by a single algebraic symbol **x**. The bold type has been used as a reminder that it is an ordered set and is different from x which the student usually expects to represent a single number or scalar. Whenever **x** is used it must of course be stated somewhere how many components it has and to which set each component belongs. If there are six components and each component can be any number, positive or negative, integer or fraction, a compact statement of this is $\mathbf{x} \in \mathbf{R}^6$. The symbol $\in$ means 'belongs to' and $\mathbf{R}^6$ is the set of all possible collections of six numbers. The objective now is to construct rules for the addition, subtraction, equality and multiplication by a scalar of these objects **x**. These rules must hold for any ordered set with any number of components. They must therefore reduce to the ordinary rules of arithmetic when $\mathbf{x} \in \mathbf{R}^1$, that is the ordered set consisting of one number only, namely when **x** is the scalar x. The student should be encouraged to obtain some or all of these rules for himself.

A valuable example of an ordered set is the representation of a point in space by co-ordinates measured with respect to fixed cartesian axes. That is, the components of the set are the perpendicular or shortest distances of the point from three fixed planes which intersect at right angles in a point, called the origin of co-ordinates. They intersect in pairs in lines called the co-ordinate axes. The student should be familiar with this idea in two dimensions and it is not difficult to extend it to three, so that it is an example in which $\mathbf{x} \in \mathbf{R}^2$ or $\mathbf{x} \in \mathbf{R}^3$. It is in fact the basic idea in the study of co-ordinate geometry. Co-ordinate geometry is the study of the properties of geometrical objects by representing points by ordered sets whose components are their co-ordinates with respect to some fixed axes. An alternative representation of a point which does not require axes to be defined is to define it by a displacement of given length and direction relative to the origin. This displacement is called a vector. If axes are defined then the vector can be represented by the ordered set whose components are the co-ordinates of the point. With a different set of axes different

MATHEMATICS

components would be obtained. The same vector can thus be represented by many different ordered sets. All the elementary rules for addition and subtraction of ordered sets should be verified for the displacement definition of a vector. It should also be shown that if a vector is represented as ordered sets (x_1, x_2, x_3) and (y_1, y_2, y_3) with respect to different sets of axes, then there is a relationship between the components of the form given as an example on page 104.

We would now like to generalize the idea of a vector so that its representation as an ordered set belongs to $\mathbf{R}^n$. Looked at another way one might ask how to generalize three-dimensional Euclidean geometry to n dimensions. The student should be able to help to discover at least part of the answer to this problem and it will prove a good opportunity to allow him to speculate and use his imagination. The vector clearly must not be *defined* as an ordered set since this is not a unique definition; many ordered sets can represent the same vector. An abstract axiomatic definition of the vector **x** is necessary, where the minimum number of postulates are stated necessary to give the vector its required properties when represented as an ordered set with n components. We define vectors **x** to be objects which belong to a vector space V. The vector space V is defined by a set of consistent axioms from which every property of **x** can be deduced. The fundamental property of V is that it consists of a set of objects or elements which can be added and multiplied by a scalar in such a way that the sum of any two elements is an element of V and the product of an element of V with a scalar is an element of V. There are eight further axioms necessary to define V completely.

The student will not find this axiomatic definition easy to comprehend. He must become familiar with the axioms and prove for himself that they are both necessary and sufficient. He should then attempt to obtain all the elementary properties of a vector space. With suitable guidance he should discover the ideas of the dimension of the space and the existence of a basis. A basis is the generalization of the idea of co-ordinate axes in co-ordinate geometry, and any vector space has an infinite number of possible choices of basis. With a given basis the vector **x** can be expressed in component form as an ordered set and it can be verified that it does obey all the rules for the arithmetic of ordered sets obtained earlier. The dimension of the space is the number of components in the ordered set. With a different basis, just as with different axes, **x** will have different components, and there will be relations connecting these two sets of components. The student should now understand that a self-consistent structure with the required properties has been constructed. To develop the idea of a structure based on axioms he should be encouraged to experiment with other sets of axioms, develop the structures that result, and see if any of them have applications to real problems.

The next concept to be explored should be that of a mathematical relationship between elements of vector spaces of different dimensions. Suppose **x** and **y** belong to vector spaces of dimension n and m respectively, that is represented as ordered sets they have n and m components, and we write $\mathbf{x} \in \mathbf{R}^n$, $\mathbf{y} \in \mathbf{R}^m$. If it is possible to associate **y** by some rule with a given **x**, then this is a relationship or, in the correct terminology, a mapping of **x** on to **y**. It is written $f : \mathbf{R}^n \to \mathbf{R}^m$ with $\mathbf{x} \in \mathbf{R}^n$ and $\mathbf{y} \in \mathbf{R}^m$.

Several examples of mappings should be examined in detail. The most valuable kind of mapping is a linear one and the concept of linearity must be discussed. The mapping f is a linear one if, given any two vectors **x** and **X** in the original space which map on to **y** and **Y** in the new space, the sum of $\mathbf{x} + \mathbf{X}$ and the product with a scalar $k\mathbf{x}$ or $k\mathbf{X}$ both map on to $\mathbf{y} + \mathbf{Y}$ and $k\mathbf{y}$ or $k\mathbf{Y}$ respectively. In mathematical notation this statement is written **x** and $\mathbf{X} \in \mathbf{R}^n$, **y** and $\mathbf{Y} \in \mathbf{R}^m$, $f : \mathbf{x} \to \mathbf{y}$ and $f : \mathbf{X} \to \mathbf{Y}$, then $f : \mathbf{x} + \mathbf{X} \to \mathbf{y} + \mathbf{Y}$ and $f : k\mathbf{x} \to k\mathbf{y}$. To illustrate it, consider the very simple case in which $n = m = 1$ and the mapping is squaring. For linearity it would have to be true that $x \xrightarrow{\text{square}} x^2$ and $X \xrightarrow{\text{square}} X^2$ implied that $x + X \xrightarrow{\text{square}} (x + X)^2$ which is false since $(x + X)^2 \neq x^2 + X^2$. This shows that squaring is not

MATHEMATICS

a linear mapping. On the other hand, if the mapping is multiplication by 4 it would have to be true that $x \xrightarrow{\text{multiply by 4}} 4x$ and $X \xrightarrow{\text{multiply by 4}} 4X$ implied that $x + X \xrightarrow{\text{multiply by 4}} 4(x + X)$ which it does since $4(x + X) = 4x + 4X$. In fact, in this illustration the only linear mapping is to multiply by a constant number. It is easily verified that the example given earlier of a relationship between the components of ordered sets (x_1, x_2, x_3) and (y_1, y_2, y_3) is a linear mapping of **x** on to **y**. Many other examples should be given illustrating the concept of linearity.

A linear mapping between vectors should then be considered in detail. With a given basis in both spaces every component of **y** can be shown to be a linear combination of the components of **x**. This means that if the components of **x** are $(x_1, x_2, \ldots, x_n)$ and those of **y** are $(y_1, y_2, \ldots, y_n)$ then the following equations hold

$$y_1 = a_{11}x_1 + a_{12}x_2 \ldots \ldots \ldots a_{1n}x_n$$
$$y_2 = a_{21}x_1 + a_{22}x_2 \ldots \ldots \ldots a_{2n}x_n$$
$$\vdots$$
$$y_m = a_{m1}x_1 + a_{m2}x_2 \ldots \ldots \ldots a_{mn}x_n.$$

This reduces to the example quoted before when $m = n = 3$. A typical number a_{ij} which appears in these equations will be in the ith equation, multiplying the jth component of **x**.

Writing down all these equations is a very clumsy notation if n or m are at all large. It therefore proves very valuable to construct a simpler language. First it is conventional to think of **x** and **y** as column vectors, that is ordered sets which are written vertically rather than horizontally as

$$\begin{bmatrix} x_1 \\ x_2 \\ \cdot \\ \cdot \\ \cdot \\ x_n \end{bmatrix} \text{ and } \begin{bmatrix} y_1 \\ y_2 \\ \cdot \\ \cdot \\ \cdot \\ y_m \end{bmatrix}.$$

Then a new entity A is defined, called a matrix, which consists of the ordered array of m times n numbers, a kind of doubly ordered set. It is written

$$\begin{bmatrix} a_{11} & a_{12} & \ldots & a_{1n} \\ a_{21} & a_{22} & & \\ \cdot & & & \\ \cdot & & & \\ a_{m1} & a_{m2} & \ldots & a_{mn} \end{bmatrix} \quad \text{or} \quad [a_{ij}].$$

It is important to notice here that, for a typical entry a_{ij}, both its horizontal and vertical ordering are important. It is in fact in the ith row and jth column. The linear relationship between **x** and **y** can now be expressed in the form **y** $= A$**x** if the 'multiplication' operation A**x** is correctly defined. The student should be able to demonstrate by reference to the detailed relations between the components that the correct rule is as follows. Any entry y_i is obtained by adding up the products of each entry in the ith row of A with its corresponding entry in the column of **x**.

Suppose now that a second linear mapping g can be defined and this can map a vector **y** $\in \mathbf{R}^m$ into a new vector **z** which belongs to a different vector space of dimension p, that is **z** $\in \mathbf{R}^p$. If we take bases in all three spaces, it is possible to write **y** $= A$**x** and **z** $= B$**y**, where B is a matrix consisting of the p times m numbers representing the linear mapping g. We thus have a repeated operation **x** $\to$ **y** $\to$ **z**, and call the mapping **x** $\to$ **z** the repeated linear mapping gf, i.e. first do f, then g. Since **z** $= B$**y** $= BA$**x**, the matrix which represents gf is just the matrix product BA. The student must verify for himself by calculating the components of **z** in terms of those of **x** that the correct multiplication rule for matrices is 'rows by columns'. That is the entry in the ith row and jth column of the product BA is obtained by adding up the products of corresponding elements in the ith row of B and the jth column of A. The general multiplication rule for matrices will reduce to the rule for column vectors given above when $n = 1$: a column vector can therefore be regarded as a special case of a matrix with only one column. The multiplication rule for matrices requires that the left-hand matrix in the product has the same number of columns as the right-hand matrix has rows. The order of the product is important and if n is not equal to m the product AB can have no meaning. This is an illustration of a situation when one of the ordinary rules of arithmetic ($AB = BA$) does not apply. Attempts should be made to construct other examples of the breakdown of the elementary rules of arithmetic.

The algebra of matrices could then be developed in a similar way to elementary algebra and examples should be given to demonstrate in which circumstances they can be manipulated exactly as though they were symbols representing a single number. It will be found that the idea of division causes difficulties that can, however, often be overcome. Examples of linear relationships between ordered sets resulting in the use of matrices should be obtained from real problems in engineering, chemistry and economics. Finally some discussion should be given of how a computer can successfully calculate the solution to such problems if they can be expressed in suitable matrix form.

The student at this stage should have constructed for himself a generalized arithmetic for ordered sets and should understand the ideas of relationships between them. He should have some ideas of the kind of problems that can be solved using these new techniques and have seen how a computer can actually obtain numerical answers. The next question to be asked is how does one generalize the elementary calculus when the variables are ordered sets rather than scalars? In other words, what meaning can be attached to the derivative of a mapping with respect to a vector?

There is not sufficient space in this article to describe in detail how the answer to this question should be obtained. It involves a re-appraisal of the definition of the elementary derivative with respect to a scalar discussed earlier. It will turn out that an alternative, unexpected definition of the elementary derivative is the correct one to attempt to generalize.

These ideas are not easy but they do constitute a generalization of such power and intellectual interest that the attempt to present them should be made. Simple cases with n and m taken as two or three should be considered in detail, as geometrical considerations will then help to illustrate and illuminate the ideas involved. Again the student should be encouraged to experiment with various mappings and their derivatives and interpret them geometrically for himself.

The principles of this general course in mathematics have been discussed in detail in the introduction. They may be summarized as follows.

1. The content should be mathematics relevant to the present day, both intellectually and in its application. It should demonstrate its power and usefulness in applications that are likely to be relevant to most of the students. It should include the development of an abstract mathematical structure as an example of ordered mathematical thought and as an opportunity to gain some impression of the aesthetic appeal of mathematics.

2. The method of teaching should be predominantly that of personal discovery by the student with some tutorial guidance.

We are not aware of the existence of a course based on these principles. We have selected the detailed content, especially the applications and the mathematical structure, from among many possible choices. We believe that many other teachers of mathematics would have made the same choice. The third part of the course has deliberately been made difficult and uncompromising. Mathematics is a severe discipline that does not accept half-truths, and this is a valuable lesson to be learnt.

These proposals are likely to prove very demanding of the student, more so than in most general courses. To comprehend unfamiliar abstract ideas expressed in unfamiliar language requires a high degree of concentration and application. It should prove a highly personal activity, and it may be frustrating for the student even though the pleasures of personal discovery are great. Two otherwise similar students may have markedly different rates of progress and many students will probably require a substantial amount of attention by the teaching staff.

The course will also prove demanding for the organizers. It will be necessary to have sufficient tutorial staff to give regular personal attention between lectures and small classes. These three forms of instruction are essential. The function of the lecture would be to present a problem and give sufficient information to enable it to be formulated. The small class, of say five or six students of roughly equal ability and a tutor, would be the forum at which the students attempted to solve the problems and argued various methods of procedure. Finally the tutorial would be necessary to discuss the student's tentative ideas and make good gaps in his background knowledge. Blockages in understanding are often caused by peripheral aspects of the central idea and it may require careful probing on the part of an experienced tutor to correct them. A typical sequence of instruction might be one or two lectures presenting a problem, then a series of classes and tutorials until the problem was solved, and finally printed notes circulated of the problem's solution and its implications, which would lead the way to the next problem and lecture. This requires careful planning and plenty of teaching staff. Aspects of the course will also require efficient computing services and programmers available to give advice to the student on writing his own simple programmes. The responsibility of the organizers is a serious one, and such a course should not be proposed lightly.

There will certainly be some drop-outs, and it would be unthinkable to make it compulsory for a student to attend. If, however, such a course succeeds for the majority of the students, and we firmly believe that it could, then something of immediate usefulness will have been learnt by each student. More valuable than this, however, is the fact that some idea of mathematical thinking and its motivation will have been given. To these students, at least, the advances of computer technology, statistical methods and mathematical symbolism into everyday affairs will no longer be mistrusted and misunderstood.

Experimental Science[1]

MICHAEL YUDKIN

MOST people, no doubt, would agree with the suggestion that non-specialist education for undergraduates ought to include some science; but it is not at all easy to specify in what way the study of science can be expected to benefit arts undergraduates. Here are three attempts to justify undergraduate courses given in different American colleges.

COURSE A. The broad objectives of the course are:

1. To provide an understanding of those phases of science which affect the individual as a person, and in family and community relationships;

2. To provide an understanding of the place of science in society;

3. To provide an understanding of the scientific attitude and method, in so far as they can serve as tools in dealing with everyday problems of living;

4. To furnish a foundation for the building of an adequate world-view.

---

1. Much of the work on which this essay is based was done during my tenure (1962–4) of a Harkness Fellowship of the Commonwealth Fund, New York. I am glad to have this opportunity of thanking the deans and members of faculty of the many colleges that I visited, from whom I had the opportunity of learning much about American practice in general education. I derived particular help from discussions with members of Amherst College, Antioch College, the College of the University of Chicago, Haverford College, Oberlin College, Swarthmore College and the University of Utah. The proposals that I make here have some features in common with courses devised at a few of these colleges.

I am greatly indebted to the many people who commented on earlier drafts of this essay.

COURSE B. The purposes of the course are:

1. To lead to an adequate understanding on the part of the student of the major facts and principles of the physical sciences;

2. To develop the ability of the student to do critical thinking in the physical sciences;

3. To develop certain desirable changes in attitude on the part of the individual student;

4. To develop in the student a sensitiveness to the social values and implications of the sciences.

COURSE C. The aims of the course are to gain:

1. Familiarity with certain present-day concepts in physical sciences;

2. An appreciation of scientific methods as a way of dealing with problems;

3. An understanding of the impact of scientific developments on society;

4. An appreciation of the readiness of the social order to accept and use scientific findings.

There are differences in style and emphasis in these three accounts, but more striking are the similarities. In fact the explicit aims of general courses in science are usually much the same. The courses are expected to teach some of the facts established by scientific investigation, to explain the working of the scientific method, and to propound the place of science in society. But agreement on ends in no way implies agreement on educational means; and the content and method of these three courses (for example) are completely different. The first centres on human physiology; the second is a superficial survey of chemistry, physics, astronomy and geology; and the third (which specifically rejects the approach of survey courses) involves historical treatment of a few physical and geological topics.

Thus we should be wary of accepting the claims made on behalf of any particular approach towards general education in science. On the other hand, in working out proposals for a non-specialist course we must have some ends in view; and in considering courses that already exist we must have some criteria for assessment.

The conventional justification of studying science refers to the importance of technology (and hence, via a logical gap, of science) in advanced societies. The man that has no science cannot understand the workings of television, rockets or hydrogen bombs. Government ministers that have to make decisions about nuclear tests may have read history, English or classics at their universities. Today's undergraduate ought therefore to study electronics and nuclear physics and thus equip himself to play an informed part in society.

The difficulty about this suggestion is that we can never know which area of science will be of public importance in twenty or forty years; most of the ministers involved in decisions about nuclear tests certainly left university before the bombing of Hiroshima. It follows that substantive subject matter – the facts that the scientific endeavour uncovers – is often of ephemeral importance, and to make it the basis of a non-specialist course will result in much time wasted. To exclude it corresponds in any case to a justifiable educational preference: one would rather teach the conceptual foundation of a subject than details culled from it.

We have seen that the explicit aims of general courses in science are often no more than vague generalities; yet, despite the apparent difficulties, I believe that it is possible to state what benefits the non-specialist ought to derive from such a course. I suggest that his needs will be best met by a course which (a) makes clear what kinds of problem are susceptible of scientific investigation and what kinds of solution such investigation can produce, and (b) provides an appreciation of the practice of scientific research, with its interaction of experiment and hypothesis.

A course that fulfils the first of these purposes will approach as near as possible to conquering the now fashionable problem of 'scientific illiteracy'. We have accepted as inevitable the fact that most people do not understand the workings of modern machinery; and it is hard to imagine an ignorance more harmless. What is neither inevitable nor harmless is ignorance about the *relevance* of science – when is it appropriate to launch a scientific investigation; what kind of evidence should we seek in solving a particular problem; how can that evidence be weighed? After all, the role of science in considering problems of public concern is not very generally understood. For instance, many people believe that the association between smoking and cancer is not 'scientifically proved'; the evidence that smoking is a cause of cancer is held to be 'only statistical' and therefore inconclusive. But a scientifically literate man would understand the way in which scientific inquiry might seek the causes of cancer, would realize that such a problem can yield only to a scientific approach, and would appreciate the value and limitations of statistics. A scientifically literate man could understand all this, and yet have no inkling of how a cancerous cell differs from a normal cell in its metabolism or microscopic appearance.

If the only function of a general course in science were to spread this scientific literacy, our task, although by no means negligible, would be fairly simple. There are conventional means of describing the functions of science and its capacity to solve problems. Lectures, discussions and tutorials, studies of historical examples and of current practice, could powerfully combine to distinguish scientific from other questions. But a course that began and ended with that distinction would be seriously incomplete. For the second and more challenging aim that I have proposed for a general course in science is to provide an appreciation of the practice of scientific research. Here we are dealing not with scientific literacy in the earlier sense – what investigations is it proper for science to undertake – but with the structure of experimental science itself. The value of scientific understanding in this sense lies in the peculiar intellectual status of science.

Science is both similar to and different from other types of intellectual inquiry. It is similar in that experimental research is an imaginative activity which requires the gift of intuition. The scientist creates hypotheses and experiments; they are not spontaneously generated from the test-tube. The more imaginative a scientist is, the subtler are his experiments and the more far-reaching are his hypotheses. But science is not all fancy: an imaginative undertaking, it nevertheless relies on experimental evidence. The evidence must be public – that is, accessible to all observers who are suitably equipped – and it must be reproducible. In these respects science differs from disciplines such as criticism of the arts that rely on a personal response to the given material.

A non-specialist course in science ought to provide an understanding of these characteristics of science; those that have finished the course should be left with an appreciation of what science is like as an activity rather than as a body of knowledge. In the following pages I intend to arrive at a description of such a course. I believe that the most useful way of defining what we want is to examine existing practice, and fortunately there are already many colleges, particularly in the United States, that teach science to non-specialist undergraduates. By describing some of these courses and seeing whether they are in any way deficient, I hope to work towards proposals for a new course in experimental science.

Although most of the 2,000 institutions of higher education in the United States have non-specialist courses in science, the majority of these fall into two classes, which could be called *Introductory Courses* and *Survey Courses*. The typical *Introductory Course* is primarily designed for first-year undergraduates intending to specialize in science. American colleges do not on the whole assume that their science specialists have a substantial scientific background from school, and so an introductory course is the first of a sequence of courses that forms an integrated programme for the undergraduate scientist. But sometimes the non-scientist is required to take such a course as part of his general education. We then find that his interests inevitably conflict with those of the specialist. The material of the introductory course can contribute towards the whole concept of the subject that the specialist will carry away from his studies; but for the non-specialist this material is likely to seem inchoate. The adaptation of the introductory course for the terminal scientific education of non-scientists is probably the least satisfactory of all attempts at providing general education.

More popular – so much so that it is sometimes regarded as synonymous with general education – is the *Survey Course*, which is designed to give an overview of the subject. A typical survey of biology, for instance, might purport to cover the whole subject in a year. It would describe the characteristics of living organisms, discriminate between plants and animals, and mention the main divisions of each kingdom. It would include an account of the morphology of some representatives of the principal groups, define a bacterium, and explain how vertebrates are distinguished from invertebrates, mammals from other vertebrates, and flowering plants from other plants. Scraps of ecology and evolution would be thrown together with an outline of parasitism and disease. If the course had a 'modern orientation', it would nod in the direction of biochemistry, genetics and heredity, and possibly even touch on cell division and differentiation.

In its justification, such a course is often contrasted with the introductory course. Teachers in a survey course appreciate that it is terminal, and they consequently select material that they believe important in the education of the non-specialist. Their conception of education, however, is quite inadequate, since it regards a university course as a means of imparting information. The philosophy appears to be that an acquaintance with a range of subject matter is itself of educational value. The result is that, although advocates of the survey course carefully distinguish it from the introductory course, both are prone to the Gradgrind fallacy. Teachers of science are particularly vulnerable to this fallacy, because science is concerned with observable phenomena rather than with judgements about abstract matters. But to learn what facts have been discovered about the observable world is not to study science. On the contrary, in the typical elementary course in science the facts are presented and learned by rote; whereas inquiry in science ought to be based on a critical attitude towards evidence, and on an avoidance of the doctrinaire and the authoritarian. Thus the claim often made for such courses that they inculcate 'scientific thinking' is the opposite of the truth.

For these reasons, several colleges in the U.S.A. reject introductory and survey courses, and have established, for non-specialist education in science, courses that discuss the principles of scientific investigation. Such colleges commonly teach a course in *Scientific Method* which derives from J. S. Mill's account of how a scientific inquiry is conducted. According to the concept that is introduced in this course, discovery in science proceeds by a sequence of identifiable steps. The scientist considers a problem, and assembles observations that relate to it. He then proposes an hypothesis to account for the observations. From this hypothesis he derives predictions that can be tested empirically. Next he conducts experiments on the basis of the predictions; if the results turn out as the hypothesis demands, they tend to confirm it; and if they do not, the new results provide a means of modifying the hypothesis.

This account of scientific research has many merits. It makes explicit the criteria that may be used to assess the value of hypotheses, and it clarifies the logical progress of scientific inquiry. But (as has been pointed out by scientists since Whewell) it is also gravely incomplete, since it glosses over the most ingenious step that a scientist takes – the creation of a fruitful hypothesis. It is at this step that the scientist displays his originality and his imaginative skill; to undervalue it reduces science to a mechanical procedure. Certainly this neglect of the creative element is understandable: intuition in science can no more easily be explained than intuition in artistic creation. But to restore the balance within the context of a course in scientific method is impossible, for it is not sufficient merely to tack on the missing piece: to state that scientific research is a creative activity does not in itself give an appreciation of what the activity is like. It is therefore a distorted picture of science that is generally presented in a course on scientific method.

This argument seems to lead towards the conclusion that a close acquaintance with the practice of scientific research itself is essential if a full appreciation of science is to be gained. Such an acquaintance with research was the central feature of the proposal by J. B. Conant for a *Case Histories Course*, to be based on extensive quotations from scientists' original papers. This course is exceptionally interesting and well worked-out, and it is worth considering in much more detail than the others that I have mentioned.

In his book *On Understanding Science*, Conant firmly distinguishes between *being well informed* about science and *understanding* science; and he therefore dismisses general education courses that impart factual information, and proposes instead a means by which undergraduates can become acquainted with the tactics and strategy of science. Tactics and strategy are displayed in the historical development of several areas of science, and Conant suggests that the study of such 'case histories' of scientific investigation should constitute a general education course in science for the non-scientist. The case histories are to be drawn from the early history of various disciplines; in this way they presuppose little factual knowledge, but they show the difficulties and confusions that are characteristic of the beginnings of a science. Conant believes that through the study of these case histories an undergraduate will come to understand the tentative groping for knowledge, the interaction of theory and experiment, the importance of novel techniques, the use of systematic observations in the formation of new concepts – indeed all the characteristics of the progress of science.

These excellent aims should certainly be the intention of any non-specialist course in science, and the techniques of a course that claims to fulfil them deserve careful study. Fortunately that study has been made possible by the publication of *Harvard Case Histories in Experimental Science*. In this two-volume series, eight case histories have been prepared in detail; each consists of extensive quotations from the scientists' original papers, together with a commentary. The series has been used in general education courses at Harvard University and elsewhere.

I shall illustrate the case history method by quoting and discussing a part of the case entitled *The Early Development of The Concepts of Temperature and Heat*. This case deals in detail with theories of heat between about 1760 and 1810; it includes a brief introduction to the seventeenth- and eighteenth-century work, and ends with a short account of the development of the subject to the mid-nineteenth century. But the bulk of the case is occupied with extensive quotations from the work of Black, Rumford and Davy, and a commentary. I shall consider the section on the latent heat of fusion of ice, based on an experiment described by Black:

... In order to understand better this absorption of heat by the melting of ice, and concealment of it in water, I made the following experiments. ...

I chose two thin globular glasses, 4 inches in diameter, and very nearly of the same weight. I poured five ounces of pure water into one of them, and then set it in a mixture of snow and salt until the water was frozen into a small mass of ice. It was then carried into a large empty hall, in which the air was not disturbed or varied in temperature during the progress of the experiment. The glass was supported, as it were, in mid-air, by being set on a ring of strong wire, which had a five-inch tail issuing from the side of it, the end of which was fixed in the most projecting part of a reading desk or pulpit.

I now set up the other globular glass precisely in the same way, and at the distance of 18 inches to one side, and into this I poured five ounces of water, previously cooled almost to the freezing point – actually to 33°F. Suspended in it was a very delicate thermometer, with its bulb in the centre of the water, and its stem so placed that I could read it without touching the thermometer. I then began to observe the ascent of this thermometer, at suitable intervals, in order to learn with what celerity the water received heat; I stirred the water gently with the end of a feather about a minute before each observation. The temperature of the air, examined at a little distance from the glasses, was 47°F.

The thermometer assumed the temperature of the water in less than half a minute, after which, the rise of it was observed every five or ten minutes, during half an hour. At the end of that time, the water was 7 degrees warmer than at first; that is, its temperature had risen to 40°F.

The glass containing the ice was, when first taken out of the freezing mixture, 4 or 5 degrees colder than melting snow, which I learned by applying the bulb of the thermometer to the bottom of it; but after some minutes, it had gained from the air enough heat to warm it those 4 or 5 degrees, and the ice was just beginning to melt. After an additional $10\frac{1}{2}$ hours, only a very small and spongy mass of the ice remained unmelted, it being in the centre of the upper surface of the water, but this also was totally melted in a few minutes more. Introducing the bulb of the thermometer into the water, near the sides of the glass, I found that the water there had warmed to 40°F. . . .

It appears that the ice-glass had to receive heat from the air of the room during 21 half-hours in order to melt the ice and then warm the resulting water to 40°F. During all this time it was receiving heat with the same celerity (very nearly) as had the water-glass during the single half-hour in the first part of the experiment. . . . Therefore, the quantity of heat received by the ice-glass during the 21 half-hours was 21 times the quantity received by the water glass during the single half-hour. It was, therefore, a quantity of heat, which, had it been added to liquid water, would have made it warmer by $(40 - 33) \times 21$, or 7×21, or 147 degrees. No part of this heat, however, appeared in the ice-water, except that which produced the temperature rise of 8 degrees; the remaining part, corresponding to 139 or 140 degrees, had been absorbed by the melting ice and was concealed in the water into which it was changed . . .

I quote now from the commentary on this passage by Professor D. Roller:

In this experiment, Black has used Martine's method of constant heat supply, the constant source of heat being the air of the room. Let us repeat Black's calculation in terms of modern units. . . . To simplify the calculation, we will assume that the contents of each glass weighed 1 lb avoirdupois, instead of 5 oz apothecaries' weight. This will not change the final result, but means merely that the room temperature would have to be considerably higher than was Black's in order for the temperature changes and time-intervals to be the same as he observed.

In the water-glass, 1 lb of water underwent a temperature rise Δt of 7 Fahrenheit degrees in 1 half-hour. Since the specific heat of water is 1 Btu/lb °F, the quantity of heat H that passed from the air into this water in 1 half-hour was

$$H = sw \Delta t = \frac{1 \text{ Btu}}{\text{lb °F}} \times 1 \text{ lb} \times 7°F = 7 \text{ Btu}.$$

For the ice-glass, the quantity of heat absorbed by its contents in 21 half-hours was 21 H, or 21 × 7 Btu, or 147 Btu. Some of this heat served to warm 1 lb of melted ice through 8 Fahrenheit degrees, this part evidently amounting to 8 Btu. The remainder, or 139 Btu, 'had been absorbed by the melting ice and was concealed in the water into which it was changed'.

This discovery of Black's suggested that it would be useful to define a new physical quantity, which has come to be called the *heat of fusion* of a substance, symbol h_f. It is defined as the quantity of heat required to melt unit weight of a solid substance without any change of temperature taking place. Thus Black's present experiment yields a value of 139 Btu/lb for the heat of fusion of ice. The modern value is 144 Btu/lb.

In considering Black's account and the commentary by Professor D. Roller, one is especially struck by the tone of assertion. One receives no impression that Black's conclusions were tentative, or that the achievement of an understanding of latent heat was slow and laborious. Professor Roller suggests that Black's experiment led him directly to that understanding. But why did Black plan the experiment? He must surely have had some earlier notion that the melting of ice requires a large quantity of heat. There is a hint of this notion in the following, which occurs in the case history a few paragraphs before the section I have just quoted:

> The opinion I formed from attentive observation of the facts and phenomena is as follows. When ice or any other solid substance is melted, I am of the opinion that it receives a much larger quantity of heat than what is perceptible in it immediately afterwards by the thermometer. A large quantity of heat enters

into it, on this occasion, without making it apparently warmer, when tried by that instrument. This heat must be added in order to give it the form of a liquid; and I affirm that this large addition of heat is the principal and most immediate cause of the liquefaction induced. . . .

If we attend to the manner in which ice and snow melt when exposed to the air of a warm room, or when a thaw succeeds to frost, we can easily perceive that, however cold they might be at first, they soon warm up to their melting point and begin to melt at their surfaces. And if the common opinion had been well founded – if the complete change of them into water required only the further addition of a very small quantity of heat – the mass, though of considerable size, ought all to be melted within a very few minutes or seconds by the heat incessantly communicated from the surrounding air.

Even after reading this account, we have no idea of how Black was led to the concept of latent heat. The observation of melting ice is commonplace: it had undoubtedly been made by many people before its importance became clear to Black. Yet there is no attempt to describe how it was that a well-known observation excited Black's curiosity. This inability to explain the awareness of a problem and the idea of a solution is not a failing peculiar to Black and Professor Roller; for we know of no way to account for intuitive discovery. Scientists sometimes claim to describe what has led them to undertake a particular investigation or to invent a new theory: in the Introduction to a scientific paper the author often attempts such a description. But these explanations always involve an element of rationalization. Black cites his observation of melting ice in explanation of his discovery of latent heat; the observation was common, but the discovery was unique.

An understanding of the tactics and strategy of science that relies on such cases is necessarily incomplete. What is worse, it is incomplete in its most vital part. The moments of discovery are the most important in science: they mark the creation of new concepts or the bringing together of observations in a new pattern. At these times the genius of a great scientist is most notable, and at these times it is most evident that science is more than a structure built by mechanical means alone. An undergraduate whose understanding of science lacks any experience of discovery will have only a skeleton in his grasp.

In making these comments I may seem to be blaming Joseph Black and Professor Roller for their failure to communicate the essence of discovery. That is not my intention; in fact the limitation of our understanding of the creative act makes the failure inevitable. Consequently the case histories course, like the course in scientific method, cannot help neglecting the imaginative element in scientific discovery. Written accounts of scientific work inevitably give it the appearance of a mechanical and routine activity.

Scientific papers generally rationalize not only the discoveries but also the progress of a scientific investigation. Written after a piece of work is completed, they give the impression that the paths of inquiry all led directly to the vindication of a particular theory. They tend to ignore the inconclusive experiment; they seldom mention the false starts and wrong turnings. They are composed with the advantage of hindsight, and in order to prove a point: they wish to make a theory as plausible as possible. They are not written in order to make clear the complex and irrational progress towards a conclusion; they generally describe experiments in logical, rather than chronological, sequence. Scientists are not usually concerned, when writing papers, to describe the steps by which they groped towards an hypothesis.

This problem could perhaps be overcome by a study of unedited notebooks, although severe practical difficulties would then intrude. But even a reading of notebooks would be inadequate in one important sense. The reader can easily become largely passive: instead of puzzling out for himself solutions to problems as they appear in notebooks, he will tend to follow the scientist's own route to his destination. To gain a full understanding of science, the gears of one's mind must be engaged; one must do work in making hypotheses; one must exercise the brain in planning experiments.

This active effort in science affords an understanding of scientific investigation which the reading of even a detailed description cannot provide.

The same objection – that the role of the reader becomes passive – can be made against the case histories course in general: a case history tends to become just another body of facts to be learned. None the less the purposes of the course were clear-sighted, and the attempts to realize them were original and ingenious. In explaining what was needed from a non-specialist course, in clarifying the difference between the gaining of information and the gaining of understanding, and in searching for material to illustrate the tactics and strategy of science, Conant has contributed in great measure to scientific education. His formulation of criteria by which general education courses can be assessed is impeccable; but the case histories course does not entirely meet them.

In the discussion up to this point, my intention has been to exemplify some of the difficulties that arise in designing non-specialist courses in science. My criteria have been: (a) Does the course make clear what kinds of problem are susceptible of scientific investigation and what kinds of solution such investigation can produce? (b) Does the course provide an appreciation of the practice of scientific research, with its interaction of experiment and hypothesis? My conclusion has been that the courses described above fail principally in the second of these aims – not because the designers of (for example) the case histories course do not have such an aim in mind, but because a mere description of the practice of scientific research cannot convey a living impression of its imaginative component.

The conclusion seems inexorable. A true appreciation of experimental science can most easily be achieved by carrying out independent investigations. Through working in a laboratory, an undergraduate can come to see how intellectual and emotional elements are intertwined in science, and can gain his own understanding of those features which an external account cannot wholly describe. He can experience what is involved in the construction of hypotheses and the design of experiments. He can come to understand the experimental methods by which theories are proved. He can assess the strength and weakness of the abstracted 'scientific method'. He can observe how hypotheses proceed to higher levels of abstraction in order to account for more varied types of observation. He can become acquainted with science as an investigative activity rather than as a corpus of doctrines.

The study of science by the non-specialist undergraduate must therefore centre on experimental work in the laboratory. At first sight there appear two obvious obstacles to this proposal – the lack of scientific background in the undergraduates, and the difficulty of equipping the teaching laboratory. The examples given later in this essay will show that these apparent difficulties can be easily overcome. But even if the lack of scientific knowledge and the technical problem of equipment are no impediment to laboratory work, the proposal that experiments should form the basis of a general education course may still seem perverse. How can non-scientists hope to compete with professional chemists or physicists in producing original research? Or is it intended that undergraduates should be set experiments like those in a school laboratory?

The practical work in this course differs both from professional research and from school exercises. Clearly non-specialist undergraduates will make no discoveries at the frontiers of knowledge; the results of their investigations will not be published in learned journals. The intention is that they should experience some of the frustration and the joy of research in science, that they should come to think and create in the same way as the professional scientist. The laboratory experience must be judged by its contribution to the education of those who take part, not by its contribution to the scientific literature.

Nor will the practical work resemble that usually done by school-children and undergraduates. Traditionally, their work in the laboratory has been designed to demonstrate facts or to teach techniques. Experiments are assigned 'to demonstrate the laws of chemical combination' or 'to show the use of the melting-point apparatus'. Instructions are provided in detail; they allow no initiative either in the experimental investigation or in the conclusions to be drawn. Indeed, there is no investigation, and there are no conclusions: the printed instructions leave no scope for the tentative approach that is at the heart of experiment and inference. Instead they describe a manipulation that must inevitably 'turn out the right way'; to follow them requires nothing beyond a modicum of manual skill and the ability to read.

In the proposed course, there will be no detailed instructions. Instead, the laboratory sessions will centre on a problem that is to be investigated empirically. The nature of the problem will be carefully explained, and the members of the class will have access to relevant laboratory equipment and materials. It will be their task to decide on an approach to the problem, to assemble the necessary apparatus, to ask for supplies that they may reasonably require, and to conduct experiments that will help them to answer the assigned question. They will be obliged to make measurements, to consider how many repetitions of a measurement are necessary, to determine the required degree of accuracy, and to do relevant calculations. Through these actions, born out of their own resources of intelligence and imagination, they will gradually acquire an understanding of scientific investigation that no passive attendance at lectures could provide.

Since the students gain scientific understanding through their own initiative, the role of the instructor in this course is delicate and challenging. He will certainly be asked for more help than he ought to give, and he will have to take care that he does not frustrate the intention of the course. He will freely provide factual information, but will be unwilling to interfere in the experimental approach. The undergraduate must come to an appreciation of scientific research by working out for himself the details of the experiments, by making false starts and turning back from them, by constructing faulty plans of investigation and correcting them. On the other hand, if an undergraduate has repeatedly failed to design a useful experiment, the instructor who refuses him all help will engender only misery. To teach in this course will require tact and a clear sense of the differences between members of the class. It will also require an appreciation of the value of questioning: by the judicious use of questions one can lead a student step by step on to the right path, and the journey will have been of far more benefit than merely setting him there.

Some of the most important sessions in the laboratory will be those devoted to discussions. After some time has been spent in working on a problem, members of the class will be asked to present orally the approach that they have used, the results that they have obtained so far, and their proposals for future experiments. All these points will be discussed by the class with the instructor, who will have this opportunity of pointing out the characteristics of good experiment. He will make clear that experimental conditions must be rigorously controlled; he will demonstrate the use of careful measurement and the place of approximation; and he will emphasize the necessity of confirming findings by repetition. In particular, he will be able to make explicit the interaction of hypothesis and experiment in the context of a familiar laboratory problem.

In making these points, the instructor may seem to be teaching a course in scientific method. In so far as the features of each investigation are common to the sciences, he will indeed be describing a special methodology of science. But the discussions in this course will be different from a conventional course in scientific method. Here they will refer to a particular investigation which the members of the class know intimately. They are concerned with the undergraduates' own experience of a problem in science, rather than appearing as abstractions from external problems. The discussion will centre on those features of experimental investigation that can be extended from the current work to scientific problems in general; but their relevance to a single familiar problem will make them more intelligible and give them more weight than the usual generalizations about science.

In addition to identifying through discussion those features of scientific research that can be readily described, the undergraduates will realize through their own experience of laboratory work that science depends for its advance on an imaginative groping towards experiments and the formulation of hypotheses. This lesson would be reinforced by their keeping notebooks in which they described fully all their experimental work and their reasons for undertaking each experiment. Such a notebook would form a valuable record of the tentative and roundabout route by which the solution of a problem is approached.

To return now to the apparent obstacles to the proposal that a non-specialist course in science should comprise a series of laboratory experiments. How can an undergraduate with little or no background in science conduct experiments without detailed instructions? Would not the laboratory have to be elaborately and expensively equipped if supplies could be demanded at will? In answer to these questions, I give two examples of problems that might be investigated during the course. The first, in physics, is relatively easy; the second, in biochemistry, rather difficult; but neither of them makes unreasonable demands either on previous factual knowledge or on laboratory equipment.

EXAMPLE 1

In investigating gravity, there are obvious inconveniences in studying the behaviour of bodies in free fall. It is far easier to study the effects of gravity on bodies whose movement is limited. For this reason, the pendulum has often been used in such studies, and observations of pendulums have contributed to our understanding of the gravitational field of the earth.

You are provided with some cord and several lumps of

metal and of wood. Make some pendulums, and determine what are the factors that affect the period of swing. The stopwatch provided will allow you to make quite accurate measurements.

When you have made some observations and found some factors that affect the period, try to construct an hypothesis to account for the behaviour of pendulums.

This problem presupposes little prior knowledge, and makes only slight demands on the resources of the laboratory. The apparatus is easy to assemble and to set up, and any additional material that students may ask for can be readily made available. It is thus quite practical for a teaching laboratory to organize such an experiment, and quite practical for an undergraduate with little or no scientific training to carry it out.

None the less the example is quite challenging, and to complete it properly requires careful thought. The value of the exercise lies in the posing and answering of many questions. Does the length of the cord affect the period of swing? Does the weight of the bob? Where should the bob be placed? Between which points on the pendulum should its length be measured? Between which points in the swing should the pendulum be timed?

In considering such questions, the undergraduate will gain some experience of the theoretical and practical difficulties that must be overcome in the conduct of scientific research. It is easy to despise the difficulties of so simple an investigation; but most undergraduates would find that several taxing problems arose during their study of pendulums. The effect of the height from which the pendulum is released will certainly seem puzzling to many, and the difficulty of making a precise estimate of the period will require them to work out a way of improving the accuracy of measurement.

The benefit to the students when they surmount these difficulties will lie not in an increased expertise with pendulums, but in an appreciation of some of the frustrations and achievements of scientific research. In addition, some of the everyday concepts that stand behind the practice of research will be made explicit through the exercises. For example, improved accuracy will come from repeating the measurements and averaging the results; and a measurement of several swings will be shown to be more accurate than a measurement of a single swing. These examples illustrate general truths about measurement on which all experimental research relies.

It will be the duty of the instructor to make conscious the principles of investigation. Some of the questions that ought to be asked about the experiment will not be asked. Assumptions will be tacitly made: most of the class will probably fail to consider whether the period is best timed from a point where the pendulum is changing direction or from a point near the middle of a swing. The instructor will then have to pose the question himself, and induce the undergraduates to consider it. One of his most important functions will be to inculcate an attitude of conscious critical questioning towards the laboratory work.

In working through such an example, the students will become familiar with the first stage of a scientific investigation – the formulation of a small-scale hypothesis. But science does not consist of an assemblage of small hypotheses. An hypothesis about the pendulum is at a low level of abstraction; if it is to be of general value, it must be fitted into a wider theory of gravitation. Later stages of the investigation would therefore involve the study of other systems in which the effect of gravitation is evident.

After the undergraduates have got what information they can from experiments on pendulums, they could be asked to investigate the acceleration of objects sliding down an inclined surface, or a system in which the motion of a falling object is used to move a toy cart across a table. For each case they could derive an hypothesis to account for the experimental observations. But these hypotheses will not be isolated exercises of imagination. In order to explain their results in each case, the students will have to consider what gravitation does. How can one envisage a force that enters into so many phenomena? What is gravitation like? How can it best be described – in physical terms? or by a mathematical model? For as a science progresses, its theory comes to encompass diverse systems; and if the students can be brought to an awareness of this increasing generality they will have learned something of great significance. During the course, then, a block of several weeks would be devoted to a series of experiments on gravitation, and during these weeks the class would work from detailed instances towards the most general account of gravitation that it is possible for them to reach.

These experiments are fairly elementary and they would probably be used early in the course. But it is easy enough to construct other series of exercises, and to arrange them in progression; and during the time allotted to the course the undergraduates could work through a number of series. Even the quite difficult problems that might be used towards the end of the course need impose no strain on the resources of the laboratory. For example, here is a relatively hard exercise:

EXAMPLE 2

The catalysts found in living organisms are called enzymes. Enzymes bring about chemical changes in the compounds on which they act (which are called substrates). A great deal of information about the way in which enzymes act can be obtained by studying the rates of reaction that they catalyse, and the influence of various factors on these rates.

One important question in enzymology is whether enzyme and substrate have to combine chemically in order for the enzyme to be active. You can investigate this question by determining the effect of the concentration of substrate on the rate of the enzyme-catalysed reaction.

You are provided with a solution of an enzyme – esterase – and with a solution of its substrate – ethyl acetate. This enzyme catalyses the splitting of ethyl acetate:

$$\text{Ethyl acetate} + \text{Water} \rightarrow \text{Acetic acid} + \text{Ethanol}$$

Study the effect of the concentration of ethyl acetate on the rate of this reaction.

When you have discovered the effect of the concentration of substrate, construct an hypothesis about the mechanism of action of the enzyme.

This rather complicated exercise can be carried out with a simple burette, a few pipettes and a stopwatch; and it makes few demands on the previous knowledge of the students. It is enough if they know that acids react with alkalis, and that this reaction allows acids to be titrated – facts of elementary chemistry taught in the lower forms of grammar schools. But in order to complete the exercise properly, several questions must, once again, be asked and answered; and it is here that the value of the experimental investigation lies. Which of the four substances in the reaction (two reactants and two products) can be most easily assayed? How can one of the four be conveniently assayed? Does the progress of the reaction affect its rate? Should the assay be made continuously, or at the end of a fixed period? Does the measurement of the reaction affect its rate? What is the rate of the reaction in the absence of the enzyme? These are only some of the questions that the undergraduates must work through in carrying out the exercise; and the instructor will make these questions explicit and will uncover hidden assumptions.

Just as the experiment with pendulums formed the first of a series of investigations of gravitation, so this study of the effect of substrate concentration would be the first experiment in a series on enzyme action. Later examples might include the effect of temperature, or of inhibitors, on the reaction. The results of these studies would all contribute towards an account of the specificity of enzymes and their extreme sensitivity to prevailing conditions, and these facts in turn could be explained in terms of their structure and mechanism of action. The previous example was intended to lead the students towards a model of gravitation; here they will be led to construct a model of enzymic activity.

EXPERIMENTAL SCIENCE

In each case the series of experiments taken together will exemplify the progress of a science towards encompassing a wider range of observations. And the differences in form between the final account of gravitation and the final account of enzyme action will also have its value. For the methods of approach of the different experimental sciences differ slightly, and it would be best if problems could be drawn from physics, chemistry, biology and perhaps other sciences. Nevertheless the processes of investigation of the different experimental sciences have great similarities. Thus by investigating several problems, undergraduates will come to know the features that are characteristic of the experimental sciences in general. The work in the laboratory will demand that they draw on their resources of intelligence and imagination; in this way their own experience – far more telling than an account supplied from outside – will lead them to an appreciation of the practice of scientific research.

I have been at pains to stress the imaginative component of scientific work, and to show how an appreciation of this component can be achieved. I have therefore concentrated, in my proposals for a non-specialist course, on describing the laboratory work that can form a part of it. But the use of imagination is not the whole of 'doing science'; and work in the laboratory should not be the whole of such a course. In experimental research imagination is moderated by critical intelligence, and is tested against results. Thus I wish to emphasize again the use of discussions and lectures to codify the undergraduates' experience of the laboratory and make clear the formal aspects of scientific inquiry. Without the work in the laboratory a conventional account of science would be abstract and difficult to grasp; but the interaction of the formal account with the experimental work could provide a profound but intelligible answer to the question *What is Science?*

The proposed course has been designed to meet the needs of undergraduates in non-scientific subjects. It is a non-specialist course, designed to make clear general principles about science rather than to teach a substantive curriculum in the sciences. But because it gives an overview of the practice of scientific research, it may be as suitable for undergraduates in science as for those in other subjects. Most undergraduate courses in science are concerned with a body of detailed knowledge about a single subject. The course proposed here would not conflict or overlap with these courses, but it would supplement them. An undergraduate in one of the sciences could acquire from it, at an early stage in his studies, a larger perspective in his view of scientific research. He would more easily appreciate from an understanding of the general features of science how the detailed structure of a single science was built up. Such an appreciation of the activity of the research scientist would be as valuable to the undergraduate scientist as to the undergraduate historian.

The proposals I make here will yield no dividend in scientific manpower. They are not intended to increase the number of technologists in Britain, and they will probably be unattractive to anybody whose sole concern is such an increase. They proceed instead from the assumption that an understanding of scientific principles and practice is possible for large numbers of people. A scientifically literate citizenry will be able to make informed choices in the many areas of public and private life into which science now enters. Scientifically literate men will appreciate the activity of the research scientist as a blend of creativity and rigorous intelligence. In a scientifically literate country, science will no longer appear as a mysterious force, uniquely powerful and slightly sinister. Scientific literacy is necessary so that man may no longer seem to be controlled by science, but may be restored to his position as controller.

Philosophy

BERNARD WILLIAMS

PHILOSOPHY FOR EVERYONE?

THERE are many good reasons for studying philosophy, but behind them all, there is the intrinsic interest of philosophical problems themselves. No one who has *no* sense of what a philosophical problem is, or who does not acquire such a sense, is going to get much out of philosophy. That sense can take different forms. It may be a feeling of puzzlement or wonder at some very general or indeed obvious feature of our thought and experience, which seems to require explanation, but which it does not look like the business of a science to explain: as that anything exists at all, rather than nothing; or that *I* seem to be something different from my body; or that we can move around in space, but not – it seems – in time. Or one may be impressed by what seems an irreconcilable conflict in our thoughts, as that all happenings (except very tiny ones) seem to be causally determined, but nevertheless we make choices. Or one may feel curious or worried about how much we know, and how; or, indeed, about how we can even think (how can some goings-on in us represent things 'out there'?). Or one may feel puzzled, confused, alarmed or in despair about more general issues of morality and social life: can anything give anyone legitimate power over another? Are questions of right and wrong just matters of convention?

Unless someone at some stage in the proceedings feels the touch of a philosophical sense in some such form, his time at philosophy will be wasted. But if he does, then it can have been worth while, even though he is never going to pursue the subject in a thorough-going or full-time way. He can have got something out of it. Not answers to his questions, perhaps, but a greater clarity about what they were; a greater ability to see several questions where originally he thought there was just one; some idea of the different approaches that have been taken to the questions, and how those approaches do or do not fit together; some liberation from the parochialism of supposing that the habits of thought of one subject or one culture are all that there are; and, perhaps most importantly of all, a grasp of the point that it is possible to attain some degree of clarity and order in one's thought even about issues which are obscure, which are not technically or scientifically decidable, and which are (in some cases) of passionate concern.

Aware, perhaps, of these possible benefits, people sometimes say that all students, or all arts students, or all of some other group of students, ought to do some philosophy. If that means that opportunities for doing philosophy should be available to them, I entirely agree. They should have a freedom to explore the subject, both by their syllabus being not too tight and restrictive to their own specialism, and by there being philosophy options which are not too specialized and deterrently professional. But if it means – as it sometimes seems to mean – that students should be made to do philosophy, I am against it. There may well be some subjects to which philosophical questions lie so close that to commit oneself to those subjects can be taken quite reasonably as a commitment to some philosophical thought, and here some philosophy can properly figure as part of the course itself: I think that at least some of the social sciences, and the law, may be of this character, and I shall say a little about this later on. But beyond the cases in which some philosophy can properly be seen as integral to the subject, the project of compulsory philosophy is surely a mistake. It is a mistake, basically, because of the point I started with, that some touch of a feeling for philosophy is essential to getting anything out of it. That feeling, though it may unexpectedly emerge, cannot be compelled, and the compelled student is not likely to find it emerging. There can be a case, with regard to other subjects, for compulsory courses which people do not much enjoy, if there is some rather tedious technical prerequisite (granted it really *is* a prerequisite) of more interesting studies later; but philosophy is not of that character, and cannot be studied in that sort of way. There is no better evidence of this than the glum, mechanical and sometimes spiritually damaging results of a compulsory philosophy course in action.

If this is so, what are the motives that lie behind the occasional demand for compulsory philosophy, and how, if at all, should these motives be realized? One motive is the desire to make people think more clearly, an educational aim which one might hope to be incontestable. Philosophy certainly can help people to think more clearly, and indeed has some special powers in this direction, since it demands rigour in argument on a subject-matter which (unlike that of mathematics) is not purely formal. But it will have this useful effect only for someone who has some commitment to it. As a general device of thought-clearing for all, it will not work. Should there, in fact, be any general device? Surely clarity of thought should be one aim of *any* academic study, and (to put it baldly) one has some right to look with suspicion at a subject which feels it needs outside help in this regard. But if there is to be any general way of encouraging people to sort things out clearly, I think that what would be appropriate would not be a course in philosophy, but a course in logic, where this would be of a fairly applied and not very formal character. The difficulty about such courses is that they are often rather trivial, and few who know any real logic want to teach them; with the result that the students may get a course which has genuine formal material in it, itself of intellectual merit, but not of much use to them. But it should not be impossible to devise such courses, which could touch on the more tempting sorts of fallacy, elementary considerations of statistics and probability, and so forth, as well as holding up for analysis confused pieces of political or critical writing, for example, and generally encouraging people to reflect on the meaningfulness of what they hear and read.

Another aim which people sometimes seek to pursue by compulsory philosophy is one probably better served by courses in the history of ideas. This is a suspect subject in this country, and it may be that it is not really any one subject. I do not feel competent to say much about its possibilities as part of general education; but I do think that often what people really want is something on the intellectual background, in historical terms, of their subjects, which might serve to bring together considerations in political history, the history of science, literature, art and so forth. Courses in philosophy could not in themselves achieve this (though they can help), and it is for discussion what sort of thing best could.

There is, however, another and more elusive aspect to these issues, which concerns the relations of other subjects to philosophical discussion. A major problem for the relation of philosophy to other subjects is provided by the ubiquitousness of philosophical questions. As soon as anyone engaged in an intellectual enterprise starts thinking with any degree of persistence, intensity and generality about what he is doing – about for instance the aims of historical inquiry, or the bases of literary criticism, or the role of experiment in a natural science – he is asking philosophical questions. There are specialized tools of philosophy which help in the discussion of such issues, and the philosophy of history, and aesthetics, and the philosophy of science have their own literature and history. This may encourage the idea of awakening students to these issues or encouraging an interest in them by way of a course in philosophy.

This is not necessarily a bad idea, and I shall later be discussing in some detail some of the ways in which it may be done. But the desired awakening is not of the literal sort that can be achieved just by making loud noises at someone, and compulsion, once more, cannot be the right idea. Behind proposals for compulsion, one might suspect – just occasionally – a motive of *shuffling off* distracting and intractable issues in the direction of philosophy; and it may be that what is pushed in the direction of the philosophy department is something which sometimes would be better done on home ground. From the student's point of view, first, these questions present themselves in their most compelling form (perhaps in their only compelling form) in the context of the other subject, and it could be that no course given by philosophers who had no direct experience of working in that subject, would have the same immediacy as a discussion of these questions 'on the job'. Though the philosopher's course may be marked by greater technical sophistication and a greater awareness of the range of philosophical issues involved in these questions, not every student will be able to benefit greatly from this, particularly in taking some brief course on the side.

The appeal to the philosophy course has implications, too, for the teacher of the other subject. If philosophical issues come into play as soon as someone doing history or literary criticism or natural science begins to think in a reflective way about what he is doing, then a teacher of such a subject who has thought reflectively about what he is doing should himself have something to say to students about these issues. There is no reason why his reflections should be particularly systematic or even, perhaps, very clear-headed; there is good reason why they are unlikely to be formed in a wide and deep study of philosophy. But they do arise out of the same experience as is prompting the questions in his students; and while he may not feel that he has anything to say on these issues to the public or to his professional fraternity, he and his students should surely have something to say to each other.

Of course, not every academic has any reflective thoughts about his subject at all; and this for various reasons. It may be for the impressive reason of total obsession, that he is so totally dedicated to his subject that he has nothing left over for general reflection about it or much else. Sometimes it is for the simple reason that he is a pedestrian and unimaginative man, doing his own subject, more probably than not, in a pedestrian and unimaginative way (it is a vulgar error that this is more common among scientists than among arts people). More interestingly, however, there is the person who feels that somehow it is not his business, that it is professionally improper, to go off into general thoughts about his activities, or, if he does, to discuss them with students. Here there is a danger of a lack-lustre timorousness being mistaken for integrity. What is needed – and of course the same considerations apply to professional philosophers – is a finer sense than we have at present of the points at which perfectly sound claims of professional integrity are overtaken by a killing professionalism, which bars one from expressing in any 'professional' context any unprofessional thoughts. In that sense of 'professional', the relations of teacher and student, even when teaching is going on, are not totally professional; or one could say, alternatively, that the profession of teaching chemistry or medieval history is a wider and freer thing than that of merely writing technical papers in those subjects. (As a rule, anyone other than a genius who could without irresponsibility publish his lectures as they were given, ought not to be giving lectures.)

Granted that not everyone is going to be doing philosophy, one hopes that many from other subjects will be attracted to doing some of it; and we must now turn to the problems involved in teaching it to them. The major problems about teaching philosophy to people not specially studying philosophy are not problems peculiar to that task: they are problems about teaching philosophy to anyone. They are problems about philosophy itself. There are certain tensions or conflicts, arising from the subject itself, which any serious teacher, or student, of it ought to recognize. None of them can be fully resolved; always something has to be given up. Giving it up – whatever, in each case, 'it' may be – can be painful or relatively painless; in either case, getting clear about what the tensions and conflicts are is necessary, if what comes out is to be a sensible and an honest enterprise. For the rest of this essay, I shall be looking at some of these conflicts.

THE SOCRATIC AND THE EXPOSITORY

Socrates is often pictured as a philosopher who had no theories, preconceptions or specialized techniques; he was just a very remarkable man of great intelligence, honesty, courage and force of character who asked searching questions, forcing people to discover and criticize their own preconceptions. The picture is not totally accurate; he may have had little in the way of theory, but he certainly had preconceptions, and he even had some techniques, if not very technical ones. With regard to those techniques, and Socrates' ways of handling a question or an argument, there were clearly things to be learned; the able young man who sat at his feet and had a number of discussions with Socrates would be clearer, see better what was happening, have better questions to ask and answers to give, in the later arguments than in the earlier ones. But – this is the point of the Socratic model – he would not supposedly have learned any new facts or doctrines or theories; he would not even, except incidentally, have learned *about* anyone's doctrines or theories. He would have been awakened to certain very general and fundamental sorts of question, about virtue, happiness, knowledge, society, and what sorts of things are worth pursuing; he would have acquired some ways of arguing about such questions, and ways of criticizing supposed answers to the questions. If he had grasped the most important, and hardest, point, that the techniques of criticism and refutation were to be applied more strenuously and searchingly to his own preconceptions and prejudices than to those of other people, he would have been Socratically educated. He would have the will towards self-understanding, and some essential tools (the more rational ones) for reaching to it. He would know, in particular, that he knew a lot less than he thought he knew at the beginning.

We have some idea, though an imperfect idea, of how to transfer the Socratic model to the teaching of philosophy now. We should not just hand out doctrines; personal discussion and argument are essential; any preconception is open to critical argument; habits of critical thought and, one hopes, a direction towards rational self-understanding are encouraged. The very general questions of a reflective character which are philosophy's concern are the focus of these free and open-ended processes. Something like this, one hopes and supposes, goes on in our universities, a good part of the time, in the teaching of philosophy.

In case the name of Socrates is invoked too complacently in connexion with these present-day activities, it may be as well to remember a few differences. Socrates was a leisured (though poor) man with leisured (and rich) pupils. They were his friends, deeply affected by his character, some indeed evidently in love with him. They talked with him if they wanted to, and because they were his friends; they were not taking a course, aiming at a degree, or fitting it all in with taking a course with somebody else. He was not doing research or sitting on the Academic Board. They talked all night while other people (some of them slaves) engaged in the economically productive activities. Though there were some books of philosophy (not many), Socrates rarely referred to them; and no one was too embarrassed about the time they might have to spend in getting to know history or geography or science, for there was not very much of these.

The hard-pressed tutor, even in a favoured university with tutors, giving his ninth fifty-minute tutorial that week on Mill's *Utilitarianism* to somebody about whom he principally knows that they are doing minor-philosophy with English, though he may try conscientiously to be as Socratic as possible, may well wonder if these conditions can possibly contain the Socratic reality.

Yet, allowing that the 'Socratic' approach is likely to be less than perfectly Socratic, we can still perhaps have some idea what it will look like in the modern university setting; and certainly there are other things with which it can be clearly contrasted. Notably, there is a purely expository approach, by which – at the extreme – lectures are merely given to a passive audience, supposedly attentive or even over-awed. The content of the exposition can be of various kinds. There is, for instance, the *Thales to Carnap* type, consisting of history of philosophy; there is the *Significant Modern Movements* type, which collects 'isms'; again, though perhaps less frequently in this country than in some others, there is *My System*, in which some revered figure condescends to expound his world-view. There is even a type of lecture, perfected by the French, which resembles all of these at once.

None of these, in itself, has much to do with teaching philosophy. The first is self-defeating. The history of philosophy without philosophy not only fails to illuminate philosophy, but even fails to illuminate its history; since it is impossible to have any living interest in the philosophers being expounded, indeed impossible even to understand what they are at, without a genuine feeling for the problems they were concerned with. This is all the more so because the interest of a past philosopher lies very little in conclusions he reached which can be detached from his work and merely reported, but in the arguments and considerations which moved him.

The same objections apply with increased force to the second type of expository lecture, which is the most objectionable of all, since it adds to the defects of the first the illusion that philosophy can be helpfully explained in terms of camps or parties (something which a conscientious teaching of mere history may, at least, be able to avoid); together – very probably – with the spurious impression that something of contemporary relevance and importance is being imparted, which cannot be so unless the student is helped to a position in which he can himself discuss the issues which move the philosophies under discussion. The third type of lecture improves on these others to the extent that the audience is confronted with someone who, one hopes, has a real concern in what he is saying, for whom it all really means something, and that can in itself be an educational experience; but its tendency to demand allegiance rather than criticism, and to produce followers rather than free men, is only one of the many objections that surround it.

Faced with these alternatives, the purely Socratic method obviously recommends itself; all the more so, when one considers that even in subjects which have a much greater and more obvious expository content than philosophy, such as history or the sciences, it is the methods of these disciplines and the kinds of question they ask which seem to be the most appropriate focus of general education, rather than a great deal of the factual content. But if a purely Socratic approach is to be favoured, then I think that there are at least three features of Socrates' practice which will have to be taken seriously. First, it will have to proceed by relatively open-ended discussion in very small groups. Second, here, above all, there cannot be compulsion; the kind of conversation that a Socratic conversation is cannot possibly be engaged in as a fulfilment of a course-requirement. Third, it is at least open to question whether such conversations need have much to do with works of philosophy, or make much reference to its history, for instance: the aim may well be best served by talking at a reflective and philosophical level about moral issues or questions of political principle, with references to philosophical writers coming in where appropriate, as will references to other sorts of writers and to works of art, political movements and so forth. The idea of 'working through a text', let alone being examined on it, is not one that comes most naturally to the Socratic relationship.

These features go, to varying extents, together. The old Scots system of making philosophy compulsory for Arts students was in its own way consistent when it made the philosophy take the form of formidably expository lectures on the history of philosophy or formal logic. A compulsory philosophical lecture, while not very philosophical, is not quite the nonsense that a compulsory philosophical conversation evidently is; and any university which seeks to combine the compulsoriness of philosophy with a purely

PHILOSOPHY

Socratic approach to it seems likely to drive both its students and its philosophy teachers into a state of hysterical boredom.

Such arrangements are a long way from a Socratic ideal. But even if one got nearer to a Socratic ideal, there would be a difficulty; indeed – and this is why there is a genuine tension here – the nearer one got to that ideal, the more evident the difficulty would become. In terms of modern philosophy, the purely Socratic approach is inadequate. This is because there are – though some outside the subject, and a few in it, would deny this – things to be *known* by someone studying philosophy. Some of these concern the history of philosophy. I said earlier – and we shall come back to the point again – that the history of philosophy without philosophy is self-defeating; but someone learning philosophy itself will need to learn something of its history, and this will involve, if it is to be useful, study of the actual writings of earlier philosophers.

Devising methods of teaching the history of philosophy demands some thought about the relation of philosophy to its history, which is peculiar. The peculiarity lies in the fact that great philosophical works of the past are still philosophically (and not merely historically) interesting, while at the same time there is such a thing as progress in philosophy. To go into this adequately would take us a long way; but I think it is worth taking a rather closer look at this peculiarity. It emerges if one contrasts the history of philosophy with, on the one hand, the history of science, and, on the other, with the history of one of the creative arts. There are several good reasons why all of us, including scientists, should know something of the history of science; in particular, to know something of its history helps one to understand rather better what the sciences are, what sort of human activity scientific inquiry is. But learning about the history of science is not itself part of learning a science, and no one would, to the purpose of teaching classical mechanics, get his students to read Newton's *Principia*. The theories, hypotheses, techniques and experiments of the past have, in so far as they are still significant, been absorbed into a body of knowledge which it is the business of textbooks to present. Great scientists of the past are known to the student of science as the originators of certain results, and not through the medium of their words. Correspondingly their results can be superseded, falsified, modified, generalized and so forth, and later theories constitute an advance on earlier ones.

In the creative arts, on the other hand, it is the work that is of primary importance, and through his own works that the artist is known. To be 'of merely historical importance' is, for both scientist and literary artist alike, to have one's works read only by historians; but to be of more than historical importance is, for the literary artist, to have one's works read by many others as well, while for the scientist it is not. Nor are works of art, in ways parallel to scientific results, absorbed or superseded. There is indeed a comprehensible historical order in the development, within one culture, of a certain art: certain works could only have come after others, and in various ways rest on their predecessors. The range of technical effects available to a later artist will typically be wider than that available to his predecessors, and the emotional range of expression may also be wider. But it would be absurd to suppose that the effect of this was to absorb the earlier work into a cumulative development, or to supersede it; earlier works do not only retain their intrinsic interest as works of art, but can stand in value, depth, and greatness fully on a level with, or above, works that follow them. The late-nineteenth-century symphony orchestra is a vastly more complex and elaborate instrument than the eighteenth-century symphony orchestra, and a wider range of things can be done with it; but this does not mean that a Mozart symphony is any the less a masterpiece, or that in appreciating a Mozart symphony we have to 'make allowances' in the light of later developments – on the contrary, it can in itself be totally satisfying. The relation of a symphony by Mahler to one by Mozart is not the same as the relation of a modern aero-engine to the Wright brothers' aero-engine; or as the relation of modern genetic theory to Mendel's.

Philosophy contrasts in this respect both with the sciences and with the creative arts. Great works of the past have contributed to advances in philosophy, and can themselves be criticized by reference to modern developments; at the same time they are still to be read and studied in their own right, and illuminated (as with works of art) by historical understanding of the situation in which they were written. The pull between these two approaches is constant, and also valuable: one has to resist the over-simplifications which would try to dump the one approach or the other. On the one hand, there is the attitude of saying that past philosophers have very often just been wrong, and their arguments, as we can now see, bad arguments; therefore we should not bother about them, but get on with our present researches. On the other hand, there are those who say that past works of philosophy are to be studied purely historically and that to import modern philosophical concepts in evaluating them is 'anachronistic'. Neither of these attitudes is adequate. The first underestimates the fact that some of the problems of philosophy are recurrent problems, concerning very general features of human thought, and that great illumination is to be had from seeing how those problems presented themselves to thinkers whose other concerns, and intellectual environment, were different from ours; it neglects, correspondingly, a valuable instrument for telling the more permanent from the less permanent; and it overlooks the remarkable extent to which each age can get something new out of great philosophies of the past. The second simplifying approach is not just impoverished, but incoherent. The historical understanding of a philosopher is, after all, supposed to be *understanding*: it is supposed to make comprehensible what he was at, what his problems and arguments were. That is not going to be done by merely repeating what he said. It involves both a philosophical sense of what a philosophical problem is, and some use of philosophical concepts and distinctions to explain (in some cases, even to translate) the philosopher's words. This already puts one in a position where one is involved in a critique and an evaluation. The attempt to do history of philosophy without benefit of later philosophy is once more, not only pointless, but impossible; the inevitable result of it is that the historian does not remain pure of philosophy, but merely deploys very bad philosophy.

Philosophy and the history of philosophy, then, are of great importance to each other. Their relation is the peculiar one by which past philosophies are both important in themselves, and yet at the same time can be criticized in the light of later developments, can be said to be in error, to involve bad argument, to have oversimplified the issue or overlooked vital considerations, to have got on to the wrong track. All these, and others, are criticisms which it will be worth making of philosophers who are of the greatest depth and importance, and indeed they are the only philosophers it is worth making them of: only philosophers that are worth taking seriously are worth refuting (at least so far as the history of philosophy is concerned). To engage in this activity, quite a lot has to be known, both of the history of philosophy, and of current distinctions, concepts and arguments.

More generally, and apart from history, there is in philosophy as in other subjects such a thing as *the state of the subject* at a given time: questions which are particularly pressing, lines of inquiry particularly promising, approaches which have been tried and need to be modified. Someone who wants to get a grasp of the subject needs to understand this situation, just as he needs to learn something of the extremely powerful and rich developments of modern logic. Anyone who tried to start totally from scratch on questions of mind and body, for instance, or problems of meaning, would be virtually doomed to recapitulate error; for while there are recurrent problems in philosophy, and some of the deepest can be seen presenting themselves in different shapes in different ages, there is no doubt at all that we have more lines of inquiry available to us than were available before, see more of the implications of various approaches and hypotheses, have disentangled more of what was confused. While there are some very basic kinds of philosophical bafflement about which we may feel that we are in much the same situation as Socrates, there are certainly a lot of highly relevant matters about which we know more than he did and about which there is more to be known; and it would be idle to deny it, and idle to devise courses which paid no respect to this fact at all. The timeless conversation is by itself an inadequate device for acquainting someone with what is in fact a going concern. Though the conversational method is essential to philosophy, and given a conflict should almost always be preferred, some respect in a proper philosophy course has to be paid to the demands of the expository.

THE PURE AND THE IMPURE

We can distinguish very roughly between certain 'mainline' areas of philosophy, such as philosophical logic, theory of knowledge, metaphysics and ethics; and areas in which the philosophical study is more 'applied' and the problems are more immediately connected with those of some other discipline or activity, as in the philosophy of law, the philosophy of history, the philosophy of religion and so forth. The latter sorts of subject typically appear in philosophy courses as subsidiary or optional subjects. We must remember that such a distinction *is* very rough, and with certain subjects there could be considerable argument about where they fall. Thus the philosophy of science is usually treated by philosophy syllabuses in this country as a specialized and optional subject, not as something which is an essential part of a philosophical education; but it could plausibly be held that scientific knowledge is such a fundamental form of our knowledge of the world that philosophy of science ought to be part of any serious philosophy course, and weak homage to this point is in fact paid by putting in some general and schematic considerations about scientific knowledge into the main-line courses, more detailed and technical questions being reserved for the specialized course.

Again, the range and content of a given subject can be treated in very different ways. If a subject called 'social philosophy' is being taught, it may include any of at least three things. It may consider very general issues about social values and the relations of the individual to society and to the state, discussing such things as political obligation, democracy, liberty, equality, and possibly welfare. Or it may concentrate on more detailed issues involving those sorts of principles: censorship, immigration, conscientious objection. Or, differently, it may embrace a subject which is sometimes alternatively called 'the philosophy of the social sciences', and consider how far the social sciences can formulate laws, the role of mathematical models, whether sociology can be value-free, in what sense anthropology gives explanations of social phenomena; and so forth. The last of these will obviously involve a good deal more in the way of technical knowledge about the social sciences than the first two do; and indeed is continuous with issues treated in the social sciences themselves – for a number of issues, it would be arbitrary whether they were regarded as belonging to 'Theory and Methods of Sociology' or to the philosophy of sociology.

In this last case, we can say that the philosophy is 'impure' in the sense that it is deeply involved with the theoretical issues, and the results, of another subject. In the second case, we can say that it is 'impure' in the sense that it is involved in the particular details, both factual and moral, of specific political and social questions. I must explain at once that in neither of these connexions do I regard 'impure' as a term of abuse. On the contrary, the attempt to keep philosophy too pure, of other subjects, or of particular cases, or of taking an evaluative side in vexed issues, seems to me to lead to futility. It is a tempting kind of futility, since it can have some very respectable motives: in particular, a refusal to set oneself up on false credentials as a *pundit*, whether it be about how sociologists should pursue their subject or how students should treat the draft. Of course, no one should set out to talk about the philosophy of the social sciences, or the philosophy of any other subject, unless he knows something fairly substantial about that subject; but he may hope to say something about the philosophy of a subject without being a full-time expert in it, and do this without pretensions of punditry. On the other issue, of moral and political commitment, I will have a bit more to say at the end of this essay.

It seems very natural if one is designing a course in which philosophy plays a minor part, to have some impure form of philosophy, a form which will be relevant to the student's main interests: philosophy of science for scientists, social philosophy for social scientists, and so forth. The reasons behind this approach are fairly obvious, and it has a lot to be said for it. The motivation for the study of philosophy will be more obvious, and more directly connected with the student's other interests; if the thing is well done, the philosophical questions will be seen to arise naturally out of the other subject-matter, and not be gratuitous; while, as an alternative, little bits of the purer parts of the subject will look fragmented, irrelevant and uninteresting. While the 'impure' approach has these advantages, it is not, unhappily, easier to do well: it is peculiarly full of pitfalls, and has the overall danger that, just because it looks so sensible and relevant, people will be all the more tempted to settle back complacently and rest on the existence of such a course without enough serious thought about what it is actually achieving.

There are several major risks. One is that, not having any general background in philosophical methods of argument or analytical procedures, the student will never in fact acquire any clear idea of what is going on. The discussions in the philosophy class may come to be seen just as the 'bull session' in which one can sound off the prejudices which are muffled, perhaps, in the more disciplined or at least content-laden parts of the course. There seems to me a lot to be said, in fact, for having opportunities for such discussions within the framework of a course (one hopes that in any place that is not dead they will go on anyway outside the courses). But if that is all that happens, an opportunity is being lost, an opportunity which philosophy should properly provide: that of encouraging a more rigorous and disciplined approach to large and general issues presupposed by the more particular specialisms elsewhere in the course. Technology and the natural sciences, as well as (in at least some of their forms) the social sciences, have a tendency to encourage in their students the idea that there are just two sorts of subject-matter – technically decidable matters on the one hand, about which you have to follow the rules of the discipline, and matters of opinion on the other, in which, roughly, anything goes. Arts subjects can also if less evidently encourage a similar view: there is a well-known type of classicist, for instance, who in practice, if not in profession, divides all questions about the classics into two classes, questions of scholarship which can be technically assessed, and the rest – 'the rest' including not only matters of taste and literary criticism, but also most of the large questions, about, say, the significance of Aeschylus's tragedies, which could make the subject of interest to an intelligent and grown-up person. A major point of philosophy, it seems to me, is to break down these dichotomies and to help to dispel the philistine illusion that the only discipline that can be exercised on thought is by a technical subject-matter. Philosophy helps people to raise questions and discuss them in a disciplined way outside the paths laid down by the techniques of a specialism. This important aim will be lost if the 'philosophy' contribution itself becomes merely an opportunity to relax intellectually from the technical discipline – although (as I have said) that opportunity is in itself something worth having.

If the 'impure' philosophy approach should miss out on fortifying a disciplined and critical approach, there is the related danger that catch-words or slogans or intellectual cure-alls will be acquired from some zealous teacher. There is specially fertile ground for these in the soggy ground on which sociology is built. It is not a criticism of sociology that it is built in the marshes: the marshes exist, and if no one builds there, they will be left entirely to snakes and bandits. But you need special health precautions, particularly against a kind of pseudo-sociological thesis which can flourish in social philosophy courses where ideology may move more freely than elsewhere. For a practical suggestion in this area, I think that the best courses in philosophy for sociologists – and the same applies to other cases as well, such as psychology – take the form of a discussion seminar given by two people, one a professional in the specialized subject who is not too technically constipated, the other an imaginative philosopher with a sceptical turn of mind who has some knowledge of and sympathy with the other subject. Unfortunately these conditions cannot always be met; and if, as sometimes happens, the specialist is too hard-line and the philosopher is too obstinate and ignorant, the results can be rather lowering.

So far the assumption has been that if we are to introduce philosophy in 'impure' applications, these should take the form of corresponding to a major concentration elsewhere in the course. In the case of the social sciences and psychology, this is probably right: there is a wealth of very important philosophical questions closely involved with these subjects, and the actual practice of them is always prone to run into them. It is far less clear that philosophy for technologists or natural scientists should preferably take the form of philosophy of science. Since I have argued earlier against people being, in general, forced to do philosophy anyway, we are principally talking about what should be offered; and while it is obviously a good idea that philosophy of science should be offered if it can be, there is also a great deal to be said for prominently offering philosophy courses centring on social and ethical issues in these cases, as a complement to the other studies, to awaken concern for the wider social implications of science, and to weaken the dreadful dichotomy I mentioned just now, between technical questions and (supposedly) 'gas' questions.

I shall not resist the temptation to add some brief remarks about other possible combinations, though they will be very dogmatic and over-general: the arguments about these in fact need to be considered carefully in relation to particular places, staff and students. In the case of students primarily historians, there are good grounds for offering something called 'philosophy of history', so long as that is firmly taken to indicate philosophical questions about our knowledge and interpretation of the past, rather than itself the canvassing of large-scale interpretations of the past. These latter should indeed be considered, and some of them given, perhaps, more serious treatment than the empiricist sniff they usually get in Britain. But the emphasis in such a course should certainly be on the treatment of historical inquiry as a form of knowledge, comparing it with scientific inquiry, considering the nature of historical evidence, and how we understand the actions and words of historical figures.

A harder question, I think, is presented by the relation of philosophy to literary studies, such as English. The obvious candidate for an element of impure philosophy in such studies is aesthetics, the philosophy of art. But this subject has its own large problems, and is spectacularly difficult to teach. It is essentially one of the most impure branches of philosophy, in the sense that anything of any value in it must be very closely related to an experience of and concern for actual works of art; one reason for the intense dreariness of most philosophical aesthetics which has been remarked by many critics, is that the writers appear not to have any deep involvement in any works of art or, if they have, scrupulously refrain from revealing the fact. To avoid this bleakness, a class in aesthetics should concern itself with actual works, but thereby runs the danger, unless very carefully controlled, of losing almost all disciplined philosophical content and turning into chat about the works. This may be merely banal; or, with more intellectual participants, it may slide irretrievably into a morass of mixed psychology, metaphysics, politics, Lévi-Strauss and autobiography. A gifted teacher who cares about the subject can avoid these difficulties, with luck, and make a great deal of it, but such teachers are pretty rare. In their absence, it may be better to look elsewhere for a philosophical link: to ethics, for example, or to an historical connexion, exploring philosophical ideas of periods relevant to the literary studies – though this too can be witheringly dreadful (there are some notorious published examples) unless well done.

We have to beware of the formula: if you are primarily studying x, then the best philosophy to study along with it is the philosophy of x. It does not follow; and, as we have already seen, 'the philosophy of x' may itself mean different things. Three special cases illustrate this further. The *philosophy of religion* is usually offered to people studying religion (some, though not all, of whom may be ordinands). Understood as a special subject, with its own history and literature, this is almost always an intellectual disaster. What should be taught to persons studying religion is *philosophy*, and quite a lot of it: this is surely one of the cases in which some main-line philosophy should be an integral part of the course. Less frequently, the *philosophy of law* is offered to those doing law. This can cover a variety of things, some of them (as exemplified in the works of Professor H. L. A. Hart) of the highest philosophical value, while others are less so. The former kinds are in no way self-contained: rather, one has important philosophical issues concerning the state, society, human action and responsibility, which are particularly relevant to the principles and operation of the law. Here again, it is certain areas of more main-line philosophy which are to the point. In fact, I think that this is a very special case, since I personally doubt whether the law, in a technical sense, should be an undergraduate course at all. It surely encourages a very narrow outlook in a profession where this is peculiarly damaging; and some of the training seems to be at the intellectual level of teaching people to reply to questions about the train time-table. What is rather needed is a 'pre-clinical' course for prospective lawyers, involving such things as history, politics and social science, and I should like to see some philosophy – not a specialized little thing called 'the philosophy of law' – as part of this. The *philosophy of education*, lastly, is a prime case in which, if the title is taken as that of a specialized subject (to the extent that it can be, for instance, with philosophy of science), it is very doubtful whether there is any such subject at all. What indeed there are, are philosophical questions and considerations likely to be of particular interest and relevance to teachers. Some of these may be specifically philosophical questions about *teaching*, but most of them will not be: they will rather be philosophical questions about society, morality, religion or, indeed, the different branches of knowledge the teachers will teach. Philosophy *of* education should rather be philosophy *for* education: and that is not primarily philosophizing about teaching, but rather encouraging teachers to philosophize.

THE CRITICAL AND THE IMAGINATIVE

Great works of philosophy display rigorous critical and analytical powers, together with powerful imagination, in the ability to see the world or the structure of human thought in a new light, to bring issues together in previously unexpected ways. In this, of course, they are by no means unique: great works of science, for instance, display the same qualities. Only the greatest works display both qualities to the highest degree, and many fine philosophers are more notable for the one than the other. Teaching the subject demands both these sorts of qualities; again, this is not peculiar to philosophy, but the nature of the subject can give rise to an unusual degree of tension between the two sorts of requirements, and demands some special sorts of choices. A teacher of philosophy is trying to encourage people to step back from what they normally take for granted, and to think about it in a critical and also exploratory way, using as much rigour and gaining as much clarity as they can. One aspect of this is to try to make people's thoughts less humdrum, to encourage imagination about how things might be different – perhaps radically different – from what they take them to be. Another aspect is to try to get thoughts into a clearer, more perspicuous and more defensible shape. There is no ultimate incompatibility between these aims, and they should go closely together; but for a given teacher, with given pupils, in a limited period of time, the pursuit of one of them may get in the way of the other. The second pursuit is that of unmuddling people, but the first, certainly in the short run, involves muddling them up. This oddness in the teaching of philosophy has been remarked throughout its history, from Socrates, who was very clear that he had to confuse people in order to enlighten them (or rather lead them to enlighten themselves), to Wittgenstein in the present day.

If you are dealing with one pupil at a time, and are of flexible temperament, and are not exhausted, and are not labouring under too tight a syllabus, the two aspects may come out rather simply by the philosophical conversation taking a very different direction with different people. It is perfectly possible (many tutors or supervisors must have done it) to spend one hour in trying to encourage some measure of pedestrian clarity and order in the thoughts of a wildly confused pupil, and the next hour in trying to induce some confusion, some sense of darkness and difficulty, some degree of intellectual alarm, in a banal or prematurely well-ordered mind. This Protean operation has its difficulties, perhaps even its dangers (one might end up losing one's own philosophical personality, like an actor), but it is certainly possible.

The tension emerges in more general terms when one has a larger group, or is thinking about syllabus and types of philosophical subject and approach for different sets of people. There are more and less meticulous philosophical writers, more and less imaginative ones, more and less wild, allusive or speculative ones; and it can be a hard question, whether one is going to make more philosophical headway in a given group by working from one or from another. Moreover, it is not always true that a work which is itself very dry and careful, or again a work which is loosely reasoned and far-ranging, will be best suited by an exposition and discussion of corresponding character. It is of course often so – to try to treat a work of Hegel by methods of the most minute logical analysis may well be a waste of time; but some less rigorous works repay very rigorous treatment, and – in the opposite direction – there is the case of Aristotle's *Poetics*, a pedestrian work, which will be worth studying only if it serves as the start to a more free-ranging inquiry.

It would certainly be a mistake for anyone to try to lay down general propositions about what aspect of philosophical activity should be emphasized in what sort of course or combination, and to what students. Patently both are part of philosophy, and essential to it; patently the emphasis varies from student to student, and with the same student at different times. Equally obviously – though it seems sometimes to be forgotten when people are talking about syllabuses – the style and emphasis of any philosophical teaching depends on what the teacher is like and what in sincerity he is capable of doing. However desirable it would be to have someone talking about Nietzsche, the first question to ask is whether there is anyone around who could talk about Nietzsche in a way which had any point to it. It will only mean anything to the students if it means something to the teacher.

PHILOSOPHY AND MORAL URGENCY

Socrates – to come back to him for the last time – taught that philosophy was concerned with the way one should live. There is a relatively painless way of agreeing with that, while allowing (what is true) that a good deal of philosophy is a very abstract and theoretical subject with no direct connexions with social or moral questions. This rests on the point, also true, that while there may be often no direct connexion, there are at least two sorts of indirect connexion: first, that the ability to think better, more clearly, and more searchingly about general issues, which philosophy encourages, cannot itself be irrelevant to a person's conduct in life; and second, that there is a connexion in the subject-matter itself, since each part of philosophy leads to others, and questions of social or individual value have their roots ultimately in issues about what human beings are, what they can know, how their thoughts correspond to reality – the general business of philosophy. To offer quick philosophical answers about questions of conduct without any commitment to the more abstract problems of philosophy is, as Plato insistently pointed out, the mark of a charlatan.

All that is true. But it carries less conviction if philosophers appear largely indifferent to political realities and moral difficulties; or the thoughts they offer about such things are merely banal; or the theoretical issues are dealt with in a way which seems to manifest and possibly even rejoice in triviality. If that is so, the critic may be inclined to think that the philosopher's activity is really a kind of evasion. Suspicious of the evasion, he may insist that philosophers should take Socrates' saying in a less painless and more direct way: that they should, much more of the time, address themselves to social and moral issues, and not in a purely analytical spirit (if such a thing is possible) but making it clear where they stand on important questions. More mildly, it may be urged that at the very least, such should be the focus of philosophy when philosophy is being taught as ancillary to other courses, where students cannot be expected in any case to go very far into the more abstract issues – here, certainly, it may be said, it must be the business of philosophy to involve people in social and moral issues.

One point must be made straight off. It is undoubtedly true that there is a lot of philosophical work, published and in teaching, which is boring and footling: just as there is a lot of research in history, or sociology, or psychology, or the natural sciences or any other subject, which is boring and footling. If anyone has suggestions for reducing the proportion of such work (with some assurance that he knows in advance what research is going to be so) it would be good to hear them. But he should not deceive himself that the way to do this is to insist that all the work should be more directly socially relevant, or express more directly social concerns. Apart from many other reasons, there is this: the ungifted bore who turns from epistemology to politics, or his equally ungifted replacement, will not be the more helpful or the less boring because he is addressing himself to social concerns; what will most probably happen is that the tedium of uninspired crochet-work will be replaced by the more odious tedium of flatulent rhetoric.

Granted this, however, it is true that one of the most valuable contributions that philosophy should be able to make in general education is in the area of moral and political discussion – even though, as I have suggested before, this is by no means the only thing that philosophy can or should do in connexion with other subjects. Waking up to thinking reflectively about what one is doing, is the most general aim of doing philosophy, and, as I have tried to suggest, there are many, and highly relevant ways of doing that. But any student who is not dead, or obsessed with his own subject, or totally sunk in an hallucinatory dream, must be conscious at this time of the bombardment of political and moral argument, and it should be the business of philosophy to have something to say to those arguments.

It will not have anything to say, however – and here criticism has straightforwardly to be accepted – unless there is a change in the predominant traditions of moral and political philosophy that have obtained for the past fifty years or more in this country, traditions which have rendered these subjects too abstract, empty and tedious. To do it better is harder than it may seem, but it must be done better. It must, for one thing, become more impure, both by being less shy of concrete cases and empirical material, and by being less squeamish about the declaration of actual moral and political beliefs. Of course, if philosophers abandon the artificial stance of a 'value-free' moral philosophy, and put their cards on the table, it is by no means the case that all the cards will be of a radical colour – some people's cards will turn out to be black ones. But at least, as students rightly say, we shall be able to see what they had in their hand.

To say finally something that can scarcely be said too often: to produce philosophical politics or ethics which discusses real issues at a grown-up level is not something you can do by just altering the syllabus, arranging the classes, drumming up the teachers, or working out the programme with the students. Unless you have capable people who care, or who can be made to care, it will come out like sixth-form civics did, dead; even if in more livid colours. And the over-riding requirement of the business of teaching philosophy to anyone is that, within the essential constraints set by a respect for the subject and the truth, you produce something which is, and is seen by the students to be, living rather than dead.

Conclusion

A. D. C. PETERSON

THE question which lies behind the foregoing essays and to which they seek, within the context of our own educational situation, to provide some material for an answer, is an old one. Since men first began to discuss the nature and purpose of education they have seen in it something more than the mere acquisition of useful knowledge or skill. This something they have called a 'liberal' or 'general' education. Yet it is doubtful if we are very much clearer what we mean by these two, possibly interchangeable, terms than was Aristotle himself, to whom we owe the first of them.

> In modern times [he wrote], people's views about education differ. There is no general agreement about what the young should learn either in relation to moral virtue or to success in life; nor is it clear whether education should be more concerned with training the intellect or the character. Contemporary events have made the problem more difficult and there is no certainty whether education should be primarily vocational, moral or cultural. People have recommended all three. Moreover there is no agreement as to what sort of education does promote moral virtue.[1]

Yet if we are to consider the proposals outlined in the preceding chapters for teaching various special subjects to 'non-specialists' in their wider educational relevance, it must be as contributions either to this old Western theory of a more general or more liberal education or to the newer Socialist theory of polytechnical education. Let us start with the more familiar.

1. Aristotle, *Politics*, VIII, 2.

CONCLUSION

The two labels 'liberal' and 'general' are commonly used interchangeably. It would be hard to differentiate, in England for instance, the fields of activity of the Association for Liberal Education and the General Studies Association; in America, on the other hand, the term 'general education' is much more commonly used, and has entered into the title of what are probably the two most important statements on the subject made since the Second World War, the Harvard Report on General Education in a Free Society and Daniel Bell's *The Reforming of General Education*, published in 1966. But perhaps before deciding on our terminology we should first consider whether the two concepts are, in practice, identical.

Historically it is clear that they have not been, if only from the fact that the opposite of a liberal education has normally been regarded as a vocational training, and the opposite of a general education, as a specialized one. In terms of contemporary usage, however, I believe that they have now come, or should have come, to mean the same thing.

When Aristotle first spoke of a liberal education he undoubtedly meant an education which was fitting for a free man, but a free man not merely in the sense that he was not a chattel slave but that he was not a 'wage-slave' either. It is sometimes said that what was essentially liberal about it was that it was an education pursued for its own sake and not for the sake of use. But to talk of 'education pursued for its own sake' is to talk too abstractly. It would be clearer to call it an education pursued for the sake of the individual being educated, as an autonomous individual, and not for the sake of some external needs, either of a master or of an employer, or of society, which he is being educated to serve.

This does not, of course, mean that those who are best educated for their own sakes, those whose education enables them most nearly to realize their own best selves, are not also those who can and do best serve the needs of their fellow-men: nor that learning to serve the needs of others, in any vocation or employment, may not in certain circumstances be the best form of educating one's self for one's own sake, and therefore a liberal education in the strictest sense. The distinction between liberal and vocational studies lies not in the content, nor necessarily in the method of teaching and learning, but in the intention. The study of law, medicine, or accountancy can be part of a liberal education: the study of Latin, Greek or theology can be a vocational one.

There is another aspect of liberal education, more modern than Aristotle, but going back at least to Bacon, which helps to fill out the concept in its contemporary setting. This is that a truly liberal education is not so much one which is fitting for a man who is, in static terms, free, but one which enables a man to free himself. This is sometimes termed a 'liberating' rather than a 'liberal' education. Where Aristotle conceived of an education which was suited to a man who was free, in the sense that he was neither a slave nor compelled by his status in society to earn a living by practising a trade, Bacon conceived of an education which would free a man from intellectual slavery to the received ideas of his time, the idols of the tribe, the cave, the theatre and the market place. This function of liberal education is particularly stressed in Jennifer Platt's essay on the teaching of sociology.

If we combine Aristotle and Bacon we arrive at a concept of liberal education something like this. It is an education which enables a man to realize, in Matthew Arnold's words, his own best self. In so far as a man's best self is, in the society we know, realized in social and economic interdependence with other men and not merely or primarily in isolation, it may include elements that are related to social and economic activity, but only in so far as these are included in order that the individual may realize himself and not in order that he may 'serve' the needs of society. Finally, it is an education which frees a man from the domination of received and uncriticized ideas or secondhand and superficial emotions, so that he may choose his own thoughts and, so far as possible, his own actions as a

CONCLUSION

morally free individual. Of course, the morally free individual may find the received ideas of his own society so repugnant that his only choice is between isolation and involvement in social revolution. It is not the function of liberal education to impose this choice, any more than it is its function to impose conformity to the norms of society. Nor is it the function of an essay on education to discuss whether the morally free individual is a possibility in the modern world or to define what is meant by a man's 'best self'. If education consists in 'bringing about planned changes in a pupil's behaviour' then the direction of those changes must be determined by some concept of the good, either of the pupil himself or of the society of which he is a member. It is a fundamental element in the concept of liberal education that it is the good of the individual rather than the good of the society which should be the criterion, and a fundamental assumption that the pursuit of the first is the best way to pursue the second.

Historically the concept of 'general' education seems to be much younger. The educational writers of the Renaissance, and, on a more sophisticated basis, Bacon, conceived of an education which would cover the whole range of human knowledge, but as both human knowledge and the educated proportion of society expanded this became clearly impossible. Encyclopaedism in the sense of a smattering of many disciplines, the vice of late-nineteenth-century curriculum planners, seems to be a delayed reaction of eighteenth-century rationalism, working on the traditional classical and mathematical curriculum of the secondary schools.

Gradually other 'subjects', first history, the great nineteenth-century discipline, then the national language and literature as opposed to that of Greece and Rome, modern languages, natural sciences, geography and finally economics have claimed a place in the secondary-school curriculum. At first these subjects were violently opposed as constituting 'an education for grocers', but as it became more and more clear that even grocers were demanding a secondary education, and that the prosperity and culture of a country depended on educating its grocers, scientists and engineers as well as its clergy and nobility, they enforced their claim.

In those European countries which had a centrally directed system they did so at the cost of diluting the old curriculum. Less classics and mathematics were taught in order to make room for the new subjects. In the end, in the extreme case, the German schoolboy was carrying on fourteen different subjects, to the end of his secondary-school career. In England, where there was no central direction, the traditional classicists succeeded in maintaining their grand old fortifying curriculum for their 'sixth forms', admitting the new subjects only as alternatives originally intended for the less gifted or socially inferior. Thus first 'modern sixths', and then 'science sixths' were added as alternative tracks, and the foundations laid for the unique English pattern of specialization beginning at the age of fourteen. In America the system of 'electives', chosen at the beginning of each year, and the principle of studying subjects either in equal and daily assignments or not at all came near to reducing the secondary-school curriculum to total incoherence, while the college curriculum was in little better shape.

It was the continental European pattern, and to a lesser extent the early years of the English pattern, which claimed as their rationale the provision of a 'general education' based on some concept of the nature of knowledge. The rationale of the American pattern, when once it broke free, in the late nineteenth century, from the European traditions, lay not in the nature of knowledge but in the interests of the pupil. But in continental Europe, *culture générale* or *allgemeine Bildung* was the avowed purpose of the secondary school, though the concept of the nature of knowledge on which it was based was not a very conscious or sophisticated one. Possibly because the new subjects had to fight for their right to be accepted as 'mental disciplines' by a teaching profession which had turned the classics into an exercise in pedantry and which paid no more attention to Huxley than it had to Montaigne, the type of general education which developed in practice was one of teaching and learning large quantities of information which was 'general' only in the sense that it belonged to a number of different school 'subjects'. If an old-fashioned education had consisted of learning a large number of Greek irregular verbs and Latin grammatical forms found once in Velleius Paterculus, a modern one cut out much of that nonsense in favour of learning a large number of French irregular verbs, capes and bays, chemical formulae and historical dates instead. Of course the best educators in the European countries protested against this confusion of general education with 'general knowledge' as they had protested against the ossification of the classics; but the growing importance of examinations, which find memorized information so much easier to test than the power of thought, worked against them. Even in the American Liberal Arts College, where a much more conscious attempt was made to break free from the pedantry, in content and teaching methods, of the European tradition, it was still widely assumed that general education could be ensured simply by 'distribution requirements' which compelled the student to absorb information in a number of different fields. By the end of the Second World War, however, the outcry against 'stuffing of the skull' had had its effect and this method of general education was widely discredited. At the same time the stresses of the war provoked a rethinking of the criteria on which the pattern of general education should be based. One of the first and most influential initiatives in this rethinking was the publication in 1945 of the Harvard Report entitled *General Education in a Free Society* and colloquially known as the 'Red Book'. Among much that now seems dated in this famous report the restatement of two great principles still stands out. The first was that the pattern of general education should conform to some objective principle, rather than simply reflect the student's transitory pattern of interests. The second was that the purpose of general education was the development of the powers of the mind rather than the acquisition and temporary retention of a mass of general information.

The authors of the Red Book found their objective principle in the understanding of and commitment to a free democratic society of the Western type. In the last days of the Second World War and the first of the peace, people were much concerned with the apparent success of the totalitarian regimes in generating commitment among their younger generation, and fearful that the Western democracies would collapse in an internal crisis of confidence. Consequently the general education which the Red Book recommended contained a large element of special courses, intended to be taken in common by all students and to introduce them to the heritage of Western culture. There was a markedly historical emphasis in its approach, not only to the social, but to the physical sciences.

To this extent the objective principle determining, for the Harvard reformers, the pattern of general education was one conceived in terms of content. As a result they found themselves involved in recommending courses which were new in content and specially designed to promote general education, rather than mere distribution requirements within the pattern of such existing subjects as were also being studied as specialisms. In this they were following the pattern of general education established in the 1920s at Columbia and the 1930s at Chicago. This divergence between special courses devoted to general education and general education sought through a pattern of specialist subjects is one which, as we shall see later, reappears again and again in systems of general education. But although the objective principle determining their pattern was one of content, it was not the mastery of content which they set as the objective of a general education. This they expressed rather in terms of the characteristics of the mind to be developed. 'By characteristics,' they say, 'we mean aims so important as to prescribe how general education should be carried out and which abilities ought to be sought above all others in every part of it. These abilities are: to think effectively, to

CONCLUSION

communicate thought, to make relevant judgements, to discriminate among values.'[2]

This distinction between the memorization of content and the development of mental characteristics is crucial and is perhaps best illustrated by examining a particular field. Let us take the study of history as an example. The old approach to the study of history, as an element in general education, was that history represented the record of what happened in the past and that no man could be called educated in the general sense if he was ignorant of at least the main outlines of this record. An Englishman, for instance, who did not know that Queen Elizabeth I preceded Queen Anne, that Rome was once the capital of Western Europe and that Canada was once a dominion of the British crown could not, according to this theory, be described as an educated man.

What was demanded here was a minimum skeleton of what Whitehead would call inert ideas. It was not required that the educated man should understand the true nature of the Roman Empire or of the Dominion of Canada, merely that he should be aware that political entities referred to by these labels once existed and roughly in what order in the general time scheme of history they existed. It was this sort of approach which gave rise to the Plato-to-Nato survey courses mentioned by J. D. Heydon which were once popular in both Europe and America and which are now so generally condemned.

There are, as the authors of the Red Book saw, very great objections to teaching history in this way. How, in a contracting world of human relations and an expanding world of human knowledge, is the range of the content to be defined or limited? If it is inadmissible to know nothing of the life of Julius Caesar, is it admissible to know nothing of the life of Akbar? If the generally educated man is expected to be familiar with the main outlines of the Russian Revolution, can he remain ignorant of the Chinese or of

2. *General Education in a Free Society*, Report of the Harvard Committee (1946), pp. 64–5.

the Mexican? More important, if in the course of his formal education the pupil is expected to become acquainted with this ever-expanding mass of superficial and pre-digested factual information, will not the ideas, being, and always having been, inert, degenerate, after he leaves formal education, into the farrago of nonsense satirized in Sellar's and Yeatman's *1066 and All That*?

More recently therefore teachers of history have maintained that the purpose of studying history as part of general education is the acquisition not of a body of information but of a skill. The educated man is not the man who is merely well informed on historical facts – Whitehead's 'greatest bore on earth' – but the man who understands how the historian recreates the past. To learn this understanding, he must study in depth some comparatively narrow field, as is suggested by J. D. Heydon, thus experiencing for himself the search for and assessment of different types of evidence, the evaluation of sources and the formation of a historical judgement. Admittedly, of course, such study in depth can only be undertaken within a broader framework of information but the nature of the framework is now determined by the needs of the depth study and not by the illusion of encyclopaedic knowledge.

This point of view satisfies the historians very much better, but it leaves open the question why the acquisition of this particular skill should be a part of general education at all. Books like James D. Koerner's *Reform in Education*, published in 1958, which plead for a return to greater concentration on the 'basic subjects' never seem to face the question of why one subject is more basic than another. Why, for instance, should acquiring, through experience, some understanding of the skill of the historian or the geographer be a more necessary part of general education than acquiring the skill of the psychologist, the social anthropologist, the architect or the accountant?

It is at this point that we come up inexorably against the need for some theory of what general education is if it is not the acquisition of general knowledge. It is only when we have some concept of the goal that we can begin to consider seriously whether engagement in a certain discipline or field is likely to contribute to it.

The Harvard Report on General Education provided a first approach to such a theory when it spoke of developing 'characteristics' or 'abilities'. As Professor Hirst of London University points out, however, in a very interesting essay[3] the characteristics are too vaguely and too generally stated to be of practical use as criteria for determining what the true pattern of general education should be. We have still no objective rationale for considering whether or how history should contribute to general education. To do this some objective principle is needed, but neither of those suggested in the Red Book is adequate.

The most fruitful line of progress seems to lie in a further clarification of the 'characteristics' of the mind. In a report on general education in the English sixth form published in 1958[4] I suggested that a general education might be defined as one which developed the powers of the mind to operate in the four main modes of human experience, the analytical (as in mathematics and syntax), the empirical (as in the social and natural sciences), the moral and the aesthetic: and that the choice of 'subjects' to contribute to general education should be made on the basis of their suitability as media for this development, and not on their content considered as information. I would now differentiate much more specifically between the methods of the natural and the social sciences, but the general approach of seeking the objective principle within the patterns of human thought itself rather than in any external pattern of content still seems to me the right one.

Professor Hirst has developed this approach much more profoundly. To summarize his argument is to do it an injustice, but it would, I hope, not be misrepresenting him

3. In *Philosophical Analysis and Education*, Archambault (ed.) (1965).
4. 'Arts and Science Sides in the Sixth Form', Oxford University Department of Education (1960).

too much to put it thus: the structure of mind, and therefore of each individual mind, is determined by those conceptual frameworks which have been worked out by the human race over centuries and embodied in a public language; is only through this public language and these conceptual frameworks that we can understand each other and make sense of our own experience; they constitute, therefore, the objective principle with which any general education must accord, and a generally educated man is one whose educational experience has enabled him to operate within the main conceptual frameworks or worlds of discourse which the human mind has framed for itself.

It is not [he writes], that the mind has predetermined patterns of functioning. Nor is it that the mind is an entity which, suitably directed by knowledge, comes to take on the pattern of, is conformed to, some external reality. It is rather that to have a mind basically involves coming to have experience articulated by means of various conceptual schemata. It is only because man has over millenia objectified and progressively developed these that he has achieved the forms of human knowledge, and the possibility of the development of mind as we know it.[5]

This neo-Kantian approach allows us the possibility of constructing a programme of general education through a pattern of studies, which Paul Hirst divides, as does Daniel Bell, into 'disciplines' and 'fields', using as our objective criterion the nature of mind itself, rather than the interests of the pupil or the demands of a chosen content. He would presumably agree with Professor Bell that these forms change with the changing conceptual frameworks of the experimental sciences.

Much still needs to be done on the analysis of the essential forms of knowledge; some would feel that the education of the emotions should play a greater part, and the whole concept is based on the assumption, as are all systems of general education, of a high degree of 'transfer'. Nevertheless this seems the only valid approach to defining what

5. Hirst, *op cit.*, p. 125.

should be implied by a 'general education'. If, then, we analyse this concept of general education in terms of its intentions rather than those of content or method, we find that it is synonymous with 'liberal' education. The pattern of studies is designed not to equip the student with a battery of skills or a range of information which will enable him to serve the economic needs of his employers, whether individuals or the state, but to develop for his own sake his capacities for rational thought and true feeling. Because there are different modes of rational thought and true feeling, a general education can be better achieved through a variety of intellectual and affective experiences than through concentration in a narrow field. It is this fact, and not the diversity of the 'map of knowledge' considered as information, which leads to the demand that in practice a general education should involve a spread of 'subjects'. If there were a single subject through the study of which the full range of a man's capacities could be as well developed as through a variety, then the study of that subject would in itself be a general and a liberal education. This was in fact the old claim of the classics, but it was a claim which was never completely valid and became less and less so the more the classics were studied for their linguistic form rather than for what the language said.

Because a general education is ideally one which develops the full range of rationality and feeling it must also be one which, at least in intention, frees the mind from the domination of received ideas and false sentiments. It seems to me perfectly reasonable therefore that we should today use the terms 'liberal' and 'general' interchangeably within the Western tradition and for convenience's sake I shall henceforth use the term 'general education' to represent the form of education discussed above. This concept of general education seems to me to correspond to the traditional criteria by which the essence of Man as Man and therefore the essential value of humanity has been determined in the Western world. The Greeks, from the time of Plato and Aristotle onwards, differentiated man from the beasts by the fact that he alone was capable of reason. They saw the essential value of humanity in the life illuminated by reason, and the purpose of education as the development of the reason. It was Rousseau who changed the course of educational thinking by differentiating Man as the one creature capable of acting freely and by positing as the purpose of education the development or preservation of the truth of feeling and the freedom and purity of the Will. Nietzsche's definition of Man as the only creature capable of making promises is only a combination of the two.

Now if Man is to be free, as Rousseau saw, he must also be rational but not merely rational, and if he is to be capable of making promises, that is extending the significance of his choices over a length of time, he must be capable of interpreting for himself the situation, or, if you prefer the word, the predicament, in which he finds himself and others. In so far as his interpretation is not his own, but the half-understood interpretation of his peer group, and his feelings not truly his own but imitative stereotypes, he is neither rational nor free. I am not talking here in terms of absolutes. For those who believe that the essence of humanity lies either in pure reason or in the absolutely free *acte gratuit*, education which is concerned with small gradual changes in the personality has little to offer. What this concept of liberal education implies is that a man realizes his best self to the extent to which he thinks rationally, feels truly and chooses freely; and that the extent of the freedom of his choice is dependent on the rationality of his thought and the truth of his feeling.

Polytechnical education, on the other hand, as developed by Krupskaya and the Marxist theorists of education, is general in a different sense. It is firmly based on a Marxist theory of knowledge which relates genuine learning to problem-solving arising out of the processes of economic production and it sees the fulfilment of the individual in the development of his capacity to serve the economic needs of society. It is general in the sense that an attempt is made to introduce pupils to an understanding of the structure of the main industrial processes on which his society is based, e.g. agriculture, petro-chemicals, heavy engineering, etc. In this respect it is not dissimilar in principle from the 'encyclopaedic' approach to general education as general knowledge which was prevalent in the West up till the end of the Second World War. The differences are that it is intended to be directly related to productive employment and that the first intention is to produce a man better fitted to serve the community. Like the theory outlined above, it provides an objective criterion by which the true pattern of general education can be determined, but it finds this criterion not in the nature of the mind but in the modes of economic production. It also makes its own fundamental assumption, which is the exact mirror-image of the Western liberal one, that is that the process of learning to serve society will also lead to the best development of the individual.

Although logically strongly distinguished, the 'liberal' and the 'polytechnical' concepts of general education produce enough similarity in practice, and give rise to enough common problems, for educators in the two traditions to learn much from each other. This is partly no doubt because both systems have been compelled to compromise with the actualities of the teaching situation, so that in practice neither is found in its pure form.

There is common agreement in all systems that a man needs both a general and a specific education, but the agreement conceals two separate interpretations of the specific element which affect the nature of the general element. The first and perhaps the most logical interpretation is that the specific element is represented by job-oriented professional education. This pattern is best exemplified in the American university system where, in the progress of most university students, general education in high school and college is followed by entry to one or other of the great graduate professional schools, law, medicine, business, engineering, etc. It is also the pattern for most students who complete higher education in the socialist systems, where a general polytechnical education is followed by professional training in one of the great institutes. The other interpretation is more commonly found in Europe. In this pattern the specific element, or specialization, is itself also regarded as part of general education and has no reference to subsequent professional life. Thus large numbers of English students specialize, both in the sixth form and at the university in history, modern languages, or English literature as part of their general education and not with any intention of becoming professional archivists, interpreters, or literary critics. In such circumstances the specific element, claiming the same intention as the general element, is more likely to encroach upon the time and commitment accorded to the general element.

Since the relationship between general and specific education is one of the most important problems arising in the discussion of general education, it will be convenient to distinguish between these two types of specific education referring to the first as 'professional education' and the second as 'specialized education'.

In general education at the tertiary level the American Liberal Arts college has undoubtedly been the pioneer in this century, though it is probable that the development of the Liberal Arts college itself in the nineteenth century owed much to the Scottish university tradition, with its early start, its four-year courses and its commitment to a broad general education in the first year. In the rest of Europe the tendency has been to assume that general education was completed in the secondary school and crowned by the baccalaureate. One result of this has been the gradual raising of the average age of transfer from secondary to tertiary education. Whereas in Scotland and America this remains between seventeen and eighteen, in Sweden and in Federal Germany it is already between twenty and twenty-one, an age at which most English students have entered on the final year of their university studies and some American students will be entering graduate school. In England and Wales, however, alone among developed countries, it is currently accepted that general education can be completed half-way

CONCLUSION

through the secondary school itself, at the age of sixteen or earlier.

Before turning to the discussion of current practice in general education at the tertiary level which is the practical theme of this book, it would be as well to consider at least in outline the previous experience of this kind which students will have had in their secondary schools before entering the university. And since we are concerned primarily with the English situation, let us begin with English experience.

The English sixth-form course has been a battle-ground between specialist and general education throughout this century. Because we, alone of European countries, had no central authority which determined the curriculum, the battle has never been decided. Professional education has never entered into this conflict and we have always accepted the assumption that the specialist element in the curriculum contributed to general education. Nevertheless a series of official circulars and reports have repeated that the emphasis given to the specialist area is too great, and exhorted the schools to pay more attention to general education. These exhortations have been repeated because they have never been effective: and they have not been effective because the examination system, which determines the competition for scarce university places, rewards specialist achievement rather than general education. Pious exhortation never has been able to counteract the pressures of a highly competitive market.

In the less than half-hearted lip service that we have paid to general education in the sixth form, we have wavered between the two patterns of achieving generality, by specially designed courses which are 'general' in their content, e.g. general studies, and by the equivalent of distribution requirements, e.g. a modern language for scientists or mathematics for the arts side.

Recent discussion of general education in the sixth form began with the Crowther Report (1959).[6] This report deplored, as usual, the over-concentration on specialist studies,

6. Ministry of Education, *15 to 18*, a Report of the Central Advisory Council for Education (England), 2 vols (1959–60).

grouped in three 'A'-level courses on either the arts or the science 'side', and also the extent to which the studies pursued in the remaining 'minority time' were neglected. It proposed no remedy, however, other than exhortation of the kind which had already failed, and it under-estimated the degree of over-concentration by refusing to take into account time spent either on home-work or 'private study' in school, virtually the whole of which should have been added to the proportion of working time allotted to the three grouped specialist subjects.

It was clear to most educators that the over-concentration and neglect of minority time were the direct and inevitable result of the G.C.E. examination system and the competition for university places. Since the Report produced no changes in these systems it is not surprising that the first two attempts to initiate any change in the sixth-form curriculum proved abortive. These were the Oxford-'Gulbenkian' attempt to organize a group of schools offering a five-section curriculum, consisting of four mixed 'A' levels and a fifth section of General Studies; and The Agreement to Broaden the Curriculum, promoted by Professor Boris Ford, which did enrol a considerable number of schools undertaking to give one third of the teaching time to general studies and to postpone commitment to either arts or science specialization at least until after the age of fifteen. The influence of A.B.C. faded out, however, in the face of competition for university entry partly, no doubt, because it had no permanent secretariat to record compliance with the agreement and no sanctions against backsliding. The next attempt at reform was more official and came from the universities.[7] Realizing that their entry procedures were responsible for premature and excessive specialization in the sixth form they proposed in 1962 a new form of entry procedure. The battery of 'O' and 'A' levels were to be replaced by 'general' and 'Course' requirements, and general education was to be tested by a General

7. Report of a Sub-Committee on University Entrance Requirements in England and Wales, Association of Universities of the British Commonwealth (1962).

CONCLUSION

Paper, to which much greater importance was to be given, a paper in the 'Use of English', and a paper in the use of a foreign language if the university required it. This change in requirements would have materially altered the balance of pressure on the schools. Something might have been made of this scheme, if the representatives of the schools had been prepared to discuss in detail the nature of the general paper. Instead, they turned it down with remarkable speed, and even violence, the reason given to me, at a meeting in Wales, being that it would favour the pupil from the large, well-staffed, grammar schools, or, even worse, public schools, which could teach for such general papers, against pupils from small grammar schools who were hard pressed to 'get them through three "A" levels'. Their opposition was reflected in a very critical report of the Secondary Schools Examination Council.[8] Gresham's Law having operated in this way, the universities' proposal sank without trace and it was next the turn of the Schools Council to tackle this intractable problem. This new body had been formed in 1964 to replace the S.S.E.C. and to advise on matters of this kind. It was clearly hoped that since it included representatives of all the bodies concerned it could formulate proposals which would not immediately be blocked by the intransigence of one or other of them. So far this hope has not been fulfilled. The Schools Council's first proposal, put forward in 1966[9] was clearly an attempt to achieve a more general education through wider distribution possibilities in conventional subjects. It accepted the view that 'general studies' should not be examined, which, on the evidence of the Crowther Report meant that they would not be taken seriously, but advocated that the division of the specialist work undertaken for the 'A'-level examinations should be divided into 'major' and 'minor' subjects. In this way a pupil taking two 'majors' and two 'minors' instead of three 'A' levels

8. Sixth Form Studies and University Entrance Requirements, Sixth Report of the S.S.E.C. (1962).
9. Sixth Form Curriculum and Examinations, Schools Council Working Paper No. 5 (1966).

would get a more 'general' education through a wider spread of specialisms, and in particular could do some serious work on both the science and the arts sides. This proposal was discussed at length and, like the universities' proposal, rejected by the schools, mainly because of the teaching difficulties involved for the smaller schools.

The Schools Council retired, thought again, and came forward in 1967[10] with a new proposal that university entry requirements should be satisfied by performance in two 'A' levels and between four and six one-year 'elective' courses, the electives being programmes designed by each school to accord with its own teaching capacities and internally assessed. In this proposal also at least one-fifth and preferably more of the time was to be devoted to unexamined general studies. This scheme which veered more towards general education through specially designed general courses was swiftly and almost unanimously rejected by the universities. Many may have seen in the electives, and the increasing emphasis on unexamined general studies, the threat of a system which had proved dangerous in the U.S.A., but the main objection was probably the difficulty of assessing the importance to be given to such non-comparable qualifications in the fiercely competitive state of university entry. The universities were fortified in their rejection by the recommendation of the Dainton Committee. This committee, set up to study the flow of scientists and technologists into higher education saw, as every other committee before them had done, that there was something seriously wrong with the sixth-form curriculum. Going, perhaps, a little beyond their brief, they included in their report (February 1968)[11] yet another proposal for its reform. This advocated bringing our pattern much more closely in line with that which is being developed in other European countries: mathematics were to be continued by all sixth-formers and

10. Some Further Proposals for Sixth Form Work, Schools Council Working Paper No. 16 (1967).
11. Council for Scientific Policy, Enquiry into the Flow of Candidates in Science and Technology into Higher Education (1968).

CONCLUSION

in addition three or four 'main subjects', so distributed as to include at least one from the three main groups of science, social studies and arts. It will be seen later that this distribution requirement is very like that in American colleges or in the International Baccalaureate.

The schools are now in the process of reacting strongly against the Dainton recommendations.

To summarize, then, in the ten years since the publication of the Crowther Report there have been six proposals for reform, two individual and four resulting from committees. Five have been rejected, four by the schools and one by the universities. It is almost inevitable that by the time these words are printed the schools will have rejected the sixth. It would be possible, of course, to take hope from the fact that a new committee, a joint one this time of the Schools Council and the universities, has started work on the problem – possible, but I think naïve. The truth is surely that any change in the pattern of sixth-form studies and university entrance examinations is going to be troublesome to the majority of those concerned and repugnant to some. As long as we assume, therefore, that no change can be made unless it has the support of all the interested parties, no change will be made. We are not likely to abandon this assumption, and therefore in considering the proposals in this book, which are concerned with the possibility of undoing at the university some of the harm done at the school, we should be wise to assume that the school pattern will remain as it is today at least for the foreseeable future. Whether it will be any easier to introduce change in the universities than in the schools is another matter, but at least we have the evidence that new courses and new combinations of courses have developed at universities over the last ten years in a way that has proved quite impossible in sixth forms.

What, then, is the pattern of education which our university entrants will have followed in the two, or sometimes three, years in the sixth? Overwhelmingly they will have taken either three science 'A' levels (counting mathematics as a science) or three arts 'A' levels. It is true that the proportion doing 'A' levels from both 'sides' has risen in the last ten years from less than three per cent to nearly eight per cent, but it is still a very small proportion and the increase may well be accounted for mainly by those who do not enter universities. Counting home-work and 'private study', they will have devoted about four-fifths of their working time to these specialist studies and divided the remaining fifth between religious education, physical education and other non-specialist work. A small band of enthusiasts in a few schools have done much in their strictly limited sphere to improve the status, content, and method of teaching general studies. But over the nation as a whole there is little reason to suppose that the situation has materially changed since the publication of the Crowther Report.

It is true that the Sixth Report of the S.S.E.C. in 1962 rejected the conclusion of the Crowther Report saying 'We do not agree that General Studies now occupy in Sixth Forms a lowly and ineffective place', but it has never been clear upon what evidence they did so. Iliffe in his research on first-year undergraduates at Keele found that at this time they were averaging three periods a week and that the accounts given of them by pupils were overwhelmingly critical.[12]

The context in which the preceding essays have been written is, therefore, different from that which prevails in any country other than England and Wales. In the other countries of Europe there is a growing tendency to greater specialization at the equivalent of the sixth-form stage, but this specialization begins later and is less intense than here. A more prolonged and more substantial commitment to general education, in the sense of distribution requirements, is universal. Consequently, although it is not uncommon in European universities to find a *studium generale*, this will consist of lectures given by the professors in the different disciplines to undergraduates who are not specializing in their subject, but who will have had a broader introductory

12. A. H. Iliffe, *The Foundation Year at Keele* (1966).

education at school. They are purely voluntary and do not affect the student's degree course. They are very different indeed from the kind of teaching of subjects to non-specialist students, who have either never embarked upon them or given them up two or three years ago, which is discussed in this book.

In the United States, on the other hand, the commitment to general education persists at least until the beginning of the senior year in most first-degree courses. Their great experience in this field has much to offer us, although the starting point and therefore the problem is so different in the two countries. The two main approaches to general education have had a long and meticulously examined trial and each still has its advocates. General education through specially designed courses has long been a feature of Columbia and M.I.T., general education through distribution requirements of Harvard and Yale; yet the total programme in each of these institutions includes an element of the other approach.

At Columbia two special courses, 'Contemporary Civilization' and 'Humanities', have played a leading part in the first two undergraduate years. Contemporary Civilization is a course designed to introduce the student to the key concepts and theories which influence the thinking of educated man today; the Humanities introduces him not merely to the masterpieces of literature, as Arnold would have done, but to masterpieces of painting and music. In the second year elective courses in such subjects as languages, physical science, anthropology, geography, etc. are bound together in a whole by interdepartmental courses in 'Oriental civilizations' and 'Man in Contemporary Society'. At M.I.T., where it can be assumed that almost all students are 'majoring' in engineering or science, between fifteen and twenty per cent of the first year's work is devoted to humanities. Courses have included such topics as 'Greek ideas and values', 'Christian ideas and values of the Middle Ages', 'Modern Western ideas and values'. This commitment to general education is carried on into the second year.

The hesitation which has often been expressed about survey courses of this kind is that the breadth of their sweep inevitably encourages superficiality, and that, because the student does not enter deeply enough into any part of the course to form judgements of his own and dispute with the teacher, they can only be taught magisterially. An examination paper from M.I.T. on the Introduction to the Humanities Course (1960) illustrates this criticism. Students were asked to reply to four questions in one hour and the questions range from 'What is the significance of the epilogue in the Tempest' to 'How does Hobbes explain the origin of speech and reason' or 'What are Locke's views on the basis of the ownership of property and how does he limit the amount of property one can own'.[13] Such questions, to be answered in an average time of twenty-five minutes, recall the questions in the English G.C.E. 'A'-level English Literature and can only encourage teaching for immediate recall of pre-digested facts or interpretations.

Nevertheless it should be remembered that the purpose of such courses is not to complete a young man's understanding of the bases of contemporary thought, but to open his eyes to where those bases lie, in the hope that he will himself, in later life, know his way around the world of intellect and pursue his own interests. Superbly taught they can perform this function, and they meet a genuine need and interest of many students; but they need to be superbly taught.

At Harvard the initial reaction to the Red Book was very much on the lines of special courses with a strong historical bias on the origins of Western democratic society, even in courses concerned with the physical sciences. There has since been a reaction against this approach, at least in science, under the influence of Jerome Bruner, who holds that the contribution of science to general education is made by doing science, not by following courses about science. The present scheme is based on a distribution requirement

[13]. Quoted in Aston R. Williams, *General Education in Higher Education* (1968).

CONCLUSION

between the three main areas of humanities, natural sciences and social sciences, but many of the courses are 'special' to general education and an attempt is made to get them superbly well taught by involving the most distinguished professors in the teaching. One of the difficulties about this, of course, is that the most distinguished professors may be prepared to do this one year, but not every year.

The purest example of general education through strict distribution requirements between the specialisms is probably the Yale programme which requires a full-year course or two half-year courses in each of the following fields: English, a foreign language, history (including history of art or of science), the social sciences, the natural sciences, classical civilization and philosophy, advanced science, mathematics or classics. This is very like the distribution requirement in the proposed International Baccalaureate (two languages, mathematics, natural science, social science and an advanced subject) a course designed for the same age group and intellectual level.

The main objection brought against general education provided solely through distribution requirements is that for economic and administrative reasons the teaching staff tend to concentrate on courses which are, as it were, part one of a specialist education and not really designed as part of general education, while the students tend to elect those courses which they think will save them time in the subsequent pursuit of their specialization. An introduction to biology considered as part of the general education of a lawyer should not be the same as the first stages of biology for a biologist.

In general the trend of development in American colleges seems to be away from survey courses, general in their content, which good students often found superficial and repetitive of what they had done in twelfth-grade high school, and towards courses which are more intellectually challenging, less wide in content and general only in the sense that they seek to develop the powers of the mind through serious work in a range of methodologies. As Franklin Patterson says of the new Chicago programme which is rather like that of Sussex:

> The basic principle is that in each field of specialization the emphasis would be on the *structure of inquiry* as it becomes manifest through subject matter. The underlying proposition is that by developing experience in the processes of inquiry in a special field, students would understand the principles of description, exposition and argument that are applicable in other subjects as well.[14]

This approach is, of course, very much in line with the concept of general education determined by the structure of the mind which was outlined earlier in this essay and to which the preceding essays in this book are most nearly relevant.

In England the first university to attempt a programme of general education on the American college model was Keele. In its strongly historical emphasis during the Foundation Year, which was intended to act as an introduction to the whole world of intellect, it echoed in many ways the intentions of the Harvard Red Book: in its distribution requirement which insisted on at least one minor subject in the following three years being taken from either the natural sciences or the humanities, it also followed American patterns. It is clear that the original Foundation Year suffered from the superficiality, over-lecturing, and excessive breadth of sweep which have been identified as dangers in America: but it was responsible for the first tentative solutions to the problem with which this book is concerned, the teaching of 'subjects' to non-specialists, and the experiment is under continuous modification.

The Keele experiment was not followed up. Nottingham University proposed, at the end of the 1950s, the establishment of a Liberal Arts college, administratively and physically independent, but within the university, whose programmes would have required work in both the sciences and the humanities, but the plan was rejected by the University Grants Committee. Since then British universities,

14. Franklin Patterson, *The Making of a College* (1966), p. 89.

CONCLUSION

perhaps following the example of Sussex, have concentrated on new courses which break down the artificial barriers within the natural sciences or within the humanities, but not between the two. A recent exception is the completely new course at Oxford in physics and philosophy. A sort of half-way house is the kind of combined course in engineering and economics or the addition of some directly relevant social study to a scientific or technological study which is recommended in the Swann Report.[15] As this report makes clear, 'Changes in schools and higher education must proceed in step', and it would be a strangely designed system of education which broadened the science courses at our universities by the inclusion of social studies, while leaving the science courses in the sixth form as narrowly specialized as in practice they remain.

The essays in this book are a contribution to the possible development of general education at our universities through a distribution requirement rather than through survey courses. In this they are probably making the best use of the European tradition. But there is much to be said for following the American example of combining the two approaches, and if we ever do derive a coherent plan for general education, either in the sixth form or in the first year of the university, courses such as these might best be combined, not only with the beginning of specialized or professional education, but with at least one general course designed to make explicit the methodology of the subjects studied and so to increase the likelihood of 'transfer'. One thing is common to the provision of general education in the U.S.A., whether in independent Liberal Arts colleges or in the undergraduate colleges of such universities as Chicago, Columbia or Harvard. It is in all cases an integral part of the degree course, and credits in general education courses are just as essential to completion of the degree requirements as credits in the major subject. There is no question of

15. Committee on Manpower Resources for Science and Technology, 'The Flow into Employment of Scientists, Engineers and Technologists' (1968).

dividing the course into a 'general' section, which is unassessed and depends for its motivation purely on the interest of the student, and a specialist section which 'counts' because it is assessed for the award of the degree. In this the American approach differs both from that of the European *studium generale* in universities and from that of most advocates of general studies in the English sixth form.

In some ways the European attitude is very attractive. We have all been sickened at times by the dominance of examinations and the pursuit of bits of paper, degrees, certificates and diplomas, rather than the pursuit of knowledge. We like to think that there is some place left in our university and school courses for the pursuit of knowledge for its own sake.

The difficulty has been that, as the proportion of the total age group who entered secondary or tertiary education increased, so the proportion of those who either wanted or could afford to pursue knowledge for its own sake, irrespective of the 'ticket', diminished. It may be that in the more affluent, egalitarian, relaxed society to which we look forward, when higher education for all will be established, this tendency will be reversed. For the moment, however, we still live in an era of fierce competition, where in this country nearly half the qualified and eager applicants fail to get a university place at all. In such conditions, where the 'ticket' is of such vital importance to the individual, it seems almost inevitable that if the course is divided into two sections, the specialized section whose pursuit leads to a good degree or certificate, and the general section, whose pursuit is an end in itself, the vast majority of students will concentrate their efforts on the specialized section. The comparative failure of 'general studies' in the sixth form to attract the degree of time and commitment, which not merely the enthusiasts but committee after committee have recommended, bears this out. So does the comparative failure of general courses, offered on a voluntary basis as part of a *studium generale* in universities.

I would hope, therefore, that if the suggestions in the

CONCLUSION

preceding chapters contribute in practice to the establishment of university courses, these will form an integral part of degree courses, and not independent 'offerings', provided on a voluntary basis, for those who can spare the time from their specialist studies.

There remains the question at what age general education should reach its culminating phase. It was pointed out earlier in this essay that in England this is at present in the fifteenth or sixteenth year, half-way through the secondary-school course, in Europe in the years between seventeen and twenty at the end of the secondary-school course and in the U.S.A. between the ages of eighteen and twenty or twenty-one in the first two or three years of college.

There is a strong movement in all three areas to concentrate this phase in the years seventeen to twenty, in American terms in grades eleven to fourteen, but to concentrate it, not in the extended school, as in Germany and to a lesser extent England and France, but in a pre-university college, as in America and, since that is what the new Gymnasium is likely to prove in practice, in Sweden. Every psychological and sociological argument drawn from the earlier maturation of adolescents seems to support this tendency. When in this country the age of majority is reduced to eighteen it is going to be increasingly difficult to go on treating eighteen-year-olds as school boys. And yet the form of education suited to their age, and increasingly to their range of ability, is not the specialized concentration in a narrow field of the genuine scholar, but the general education of the college student, who may or may not proceed at a later stage to a life of scholarship. I would hope, therefore, that the essays in this book, though initially contributing to the broadening of undergraduate courses in our universities, might in time provide some ideas for courses in the 'Liberal Arts', 'Sixth Form' or 'General' colleges of the future.